AT THE SOURCE

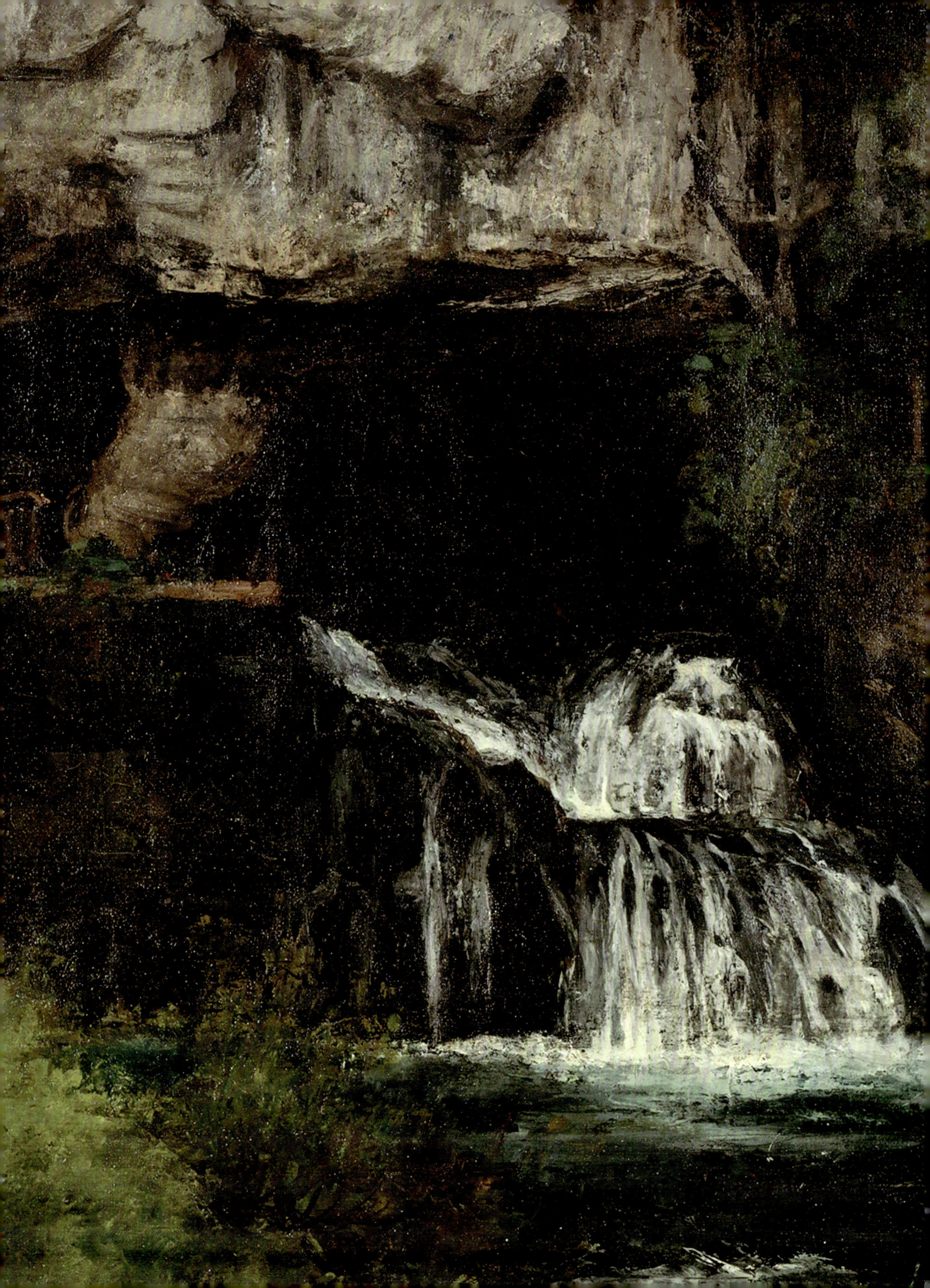

AT THE SOURCE

A COURBET LANDSCAPE REDISCOVERED

EDITED BY

André Dombrowski and Lynn Marsden-Atlass

WITH ESSAYS BY

Jalen Chang

Petra ten-Doesschate Chu

André Dombrowski

Aruna D'Souza

Adam C. Finnefrock

Paul Galvez

Lynn Marsden-Atlass

Jennifer L. Mass

Mary Morton

Emily Zimmerman

ARTHUR ROSS GALLERY
UNIVERSITY OF PENNSYLVANIA, PHILADELPHIA

DISTRIBUTED BY
THE UNIVERSITY OF PENNSYLVANIA PRESS

Published on the occasion of the exhibition *At the Source: A Courbet Landscape Rediscovered* at the Arthur Ross Gallery, curated by Lynn Marsden-Atlass, Executive Director of the Arthur Ross Gallery and University Curator, and André Dombrowski, Frances Shapiro-Weitzenhoffer Associate Professor of 19th-Century European Art at the University of Pennsylvania, on view February 4–May 28, 2023.

Generous support from Arthur Ross Gallery Advisory Board member Betsy Scott Kleeblatt (CW'68) and the Philadelphia Cultural Fund made this catalogue possible. Additional support for the exhibition at the Arthur Ross Gallery is provided by the J & AR Foundation, the Connelly Foundation, the Dolfinger-McMahon Foundation, the David J. Evans Exhibition Fund, Dean Mark S. Wolff and Penn Dental Medicine, Friends of the Arthur Ross Gallery, the Pennsylvania Council on the Arts, and the University of Pennsylvania Department of History of Art.

Copyright © 2023 Arthur Ross Gallery, University of Pennsylvania
220 S. 34th Street
Philadelphia, PA 19104-6303
ArthurRossGallery.org

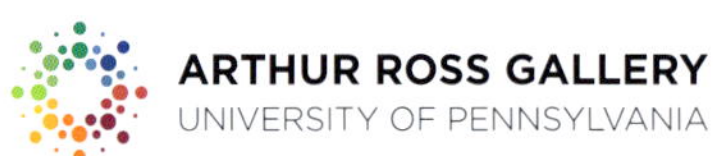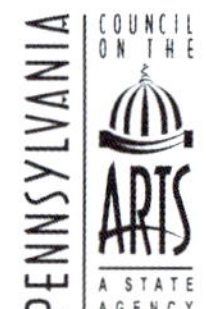

ISBN: 978-1-7347338-4-6
Library of Congress Control Number: 2022920073

Edited by Kristin Swan
Designed by Cooper Graphic Design
Printed by Brilliant Graphics

FRONT COVER: Gustave Courbet, *The Source of the Lison*, 1864 (detail), oil on canvas, 18 ½ × 22 in. (47 × 55.9 cm). University of Pennsylvania Art Collection, Gift of Thomas W. Evans, 1912.0005.0237.

BACK COVER: James Duffield Harding, *Source of the Lison* (detail), lithograph from Charles Nodier, Isidore-Justin-Séverin Taylor, and Achille-Alexandre-Alphonse de Cailloux de Cailleux, *Voyages pittoresques et romantiques dans l'ancienne France*, vol. 2, *Franche-Comté* (Paris: P. Didot l'aîné, 1825), pl. 117. Cleveland Art Museum: Twenty-fifth anniversary gift, Mr. and Mrs. Lewis B. Williams Collection, 1941.162.

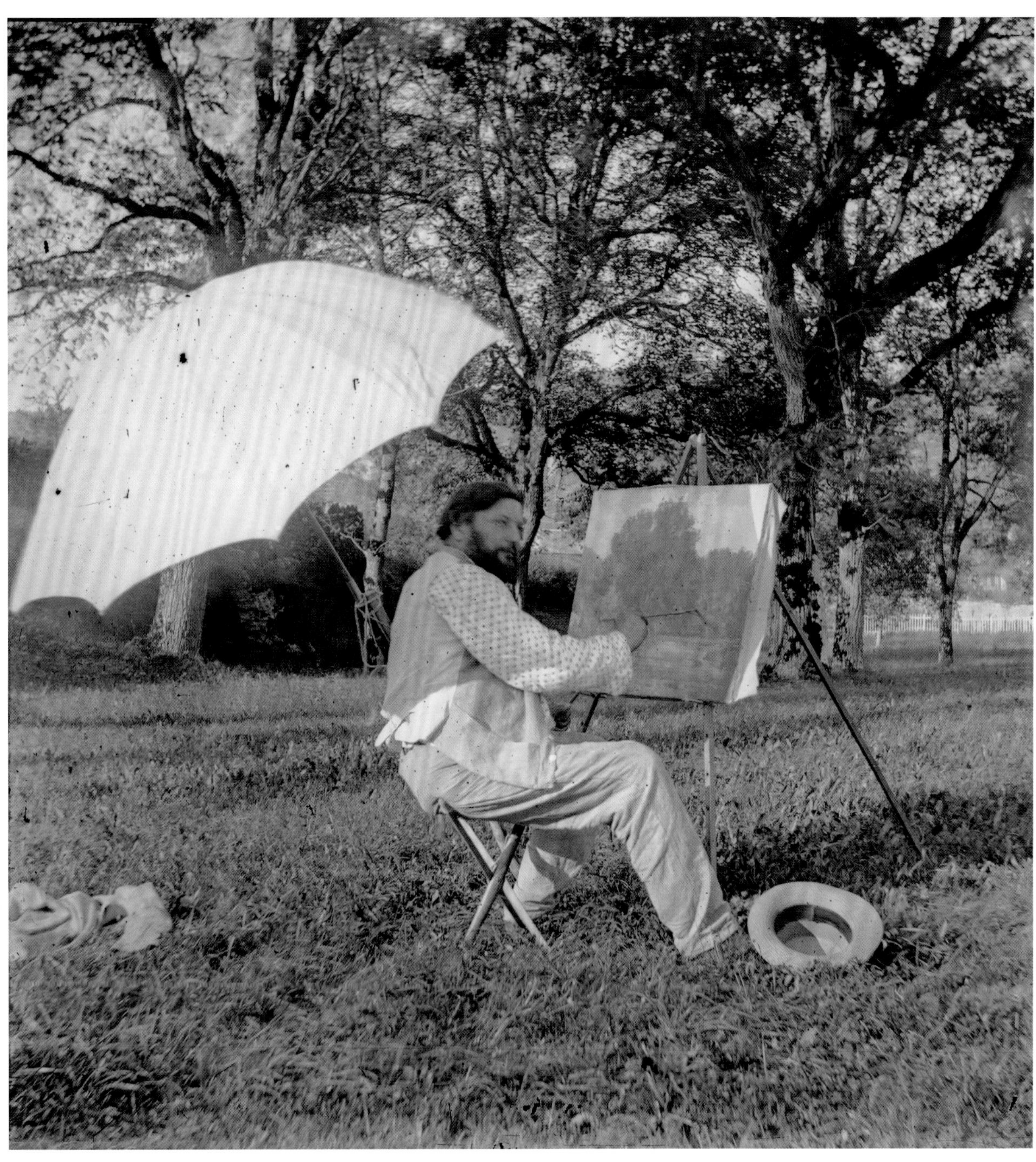

ABOVE Eugène Feyen, *Gustave Courbet Painting in His Field, June 1864,* 1864, photograph after a stereoscopic plate. Musée Courbet, Ornans.

CONTENTS

ix Foreword
LYNN MARSDEN-ATLASS

x Acknowledgments
LYNN MARSDEN-ATLASS AND ANDRÉ DOMBROWSKI

1 Introduction
ANDRÉ DOMBROWSKI

9 Thomas W. Evans: A Gilded Life and Legacy
LYNN MARSDEN-ATLASS

21 Courbet and the Source of the Lison:
Geological Curiosity, Industrial Power Source,
and "Natural Site of an Artistic Character"
PETRA TEN-DOESSCHATE CHU

33 Of Sources and Salt
PAUL GALVEZ

47 Courbet Painting in Nature
MARY MORTON

59 Paths to the Source: The Lison and
Nineteenth-Century Tourism
JALEN CHANG

67   Source, Origin, Endpoint, Projection, Possession
ARUNA D'SOUZA

75   Displays of Power: Courbet as Exhibition Maker
EMILY ZIMMERMAN

81   Courbet, or Not Courbet, That Is the Question
PETRA TEN-DOESSCHATE CHU

99   Unsettled Ground: The Development of Courbet
Landscape Studies
JALEN CHANG

105   Pigment Analysis of a Landscape by
Gustave Courbet
ADAM C. FINNEFROCK AND JENNIFER L. MASS

109   Courbet in Context

112   Exhibition Checklist

120   Further Reading

123   Contributors

127   Photography Credits

FOREWORD

Sparked by the discovery of a Gustave Courbet painting depicting the source of the French Lison River in the University of Pennsylvania's art collection, *At the Source: A Courbet Landscape Rediscovered* (February 4–May 28, 2023) showcases the infamous painter's modern landscape practice. Focusing on the motifs of grottos and waterfalls in his art of the 1850s and 1860s, the exhibition highlights the university's newly rediscovered Courbet painting, not shown in public for close to one hundred years, emphasizing the process of authenticating and conserving this historic work.

Published on the occasion of the fortieth anniversary of the Arthur Ross Gallery, the accompanying catalogue brings together new essays by leading Courbet scholars, including Petra ten Doesschate Chu, Paul Galvez, Mary Morton, and Aruna D'Souza, among others. These texts consider Courbet's modern landscapes within the genre of nineteenth-century landscape painting and in relation to other artists' depictions of the source of the Lison, while drawing connections to Courbet's political activism, his interests in geology and environmentalism, as well as his engagement with issues of gender.

With gratitude, this exhibition is dedicated to Arthur (1910–2007) and Janet Ross. At forty, the Arthur Ross Gallery continues to be open and free to all.

LYNN MARSDEN-ATLASS
Executive Director, Arthur Ross Gallery, and University Curator

ACKNOWLEDGMENTS

In celebration of the Arthur Ross Gallery's fortieth anniversary, we are proud to present *At the Source: A Courbet Landscape Rediscovered* and its accompanying catalogue. It has been a fascinating journey over nearly six years to realize this exhibition, and we owe our sincerest thanks to the many individuals who have been essential to this process.

First, we would like to thank the lenders to the exhibition: Petra ten-Doesschate Chu; the Kislak Center for Special Collections, Rare Books and Manuscripts, University of Pennsylvania; the National Gallery of Art Library; a Private Collector, Minnesota Marine Art Museum, Winona, Minnesota; the Philadelphia Museum of Art; the Yale University Art Gallery; and the University of Pennsylvania Art Collection.

Arthur Ross Gallery Advisory Board member Betsy Scott Kleeblatt (CW'68) provided generous support for the exhibition catalogue, in honor of André Dombrowski, as did the Philadelphia Cultural Fund. We also thank Mark S. Wolff, Morton Amsterdam Dean of Penn Dental Medicine, for supporting the exhibition, as well as Elizabeth Ketterlinus (PDM), who has worked with the Office of the Curator since 2010 on the conservation and legacy of the Thomas W. Evans Collection. Additional support for the exhibition comes from the J & AR Foundation, the Connelly Foundation, the Dolfinger-McMahon Foundation, the David J. Evans Exhibition Fund, the Pennsylvania Council on the Arts, Friends of the Arthur Ross Gallery, and the University of Pennsylvania Department of History of Art.

We would like to personally thank the following scholars for generously sharing their expertise on Courbet's landscapes and for their important contributions to this exhibition catalogue:

Petra ten-Doesschate Chu, Aruna D'Souza, Paul Galvez, and Mary Morton. Ségolène Le Men also kindly agreed to share her thoughts on the painting with us. Jalen Chang, PhD candidate in the history of art at the University of Pennsylvania, has provided valuable research and scholarship and deserves our thanks. Jennifer L. Mass and Adam C. Finnefrock of Scientific Analysis of Fine Art, LLC, have allowed us to publish part of their 2018 report on the painting at the heart of this project. Emily Zimmerman, who joined the staff of the Arthur Ross Gallery last April as assistant director, deserves special thanks as both a contributor to and project manager of this publication. Furthermore, we are very grateful to Sébastien Fernier, the Comité Courbet, and the Institut Gustave Courbet in Ornans for their insights.

We also extend our sincere thanks to Interim Provost Beth Winkelstein, Mark Dingfield, and the Arthur Ross Gallery Advisory Board for their support. We are grateful to the many individuals who have contributed to the realization of this exhibition and catalogue, including Michele Cooper, Daniel Murphy, Raymond Rorke, Kristin Swan, John Taylor, John Junius Taylor, and Gerhardt Koerner. Additional thanks go to Mary Francis and Penn Press for the catalogue's worldwide distribution.

Finally, our deep appreciation is due to the talented staff at the Arthur Ross Gallery and Office of the Curator who have been involved in all aspects of the exhibition and publication: Lynn Smith Dolby, Elizabeth McClafferty, Sara Stewart, and Emily Zimmerman.

LYNN MARSDEN-ATLASS

Executive Director, Arthur Ross Gallery, and University Curator

ANDRÉ DOMBROWSKI

Frances Shapiro-Weitzenhoffer Associate Professor of 19th-Century European Art, Department of the History of Art

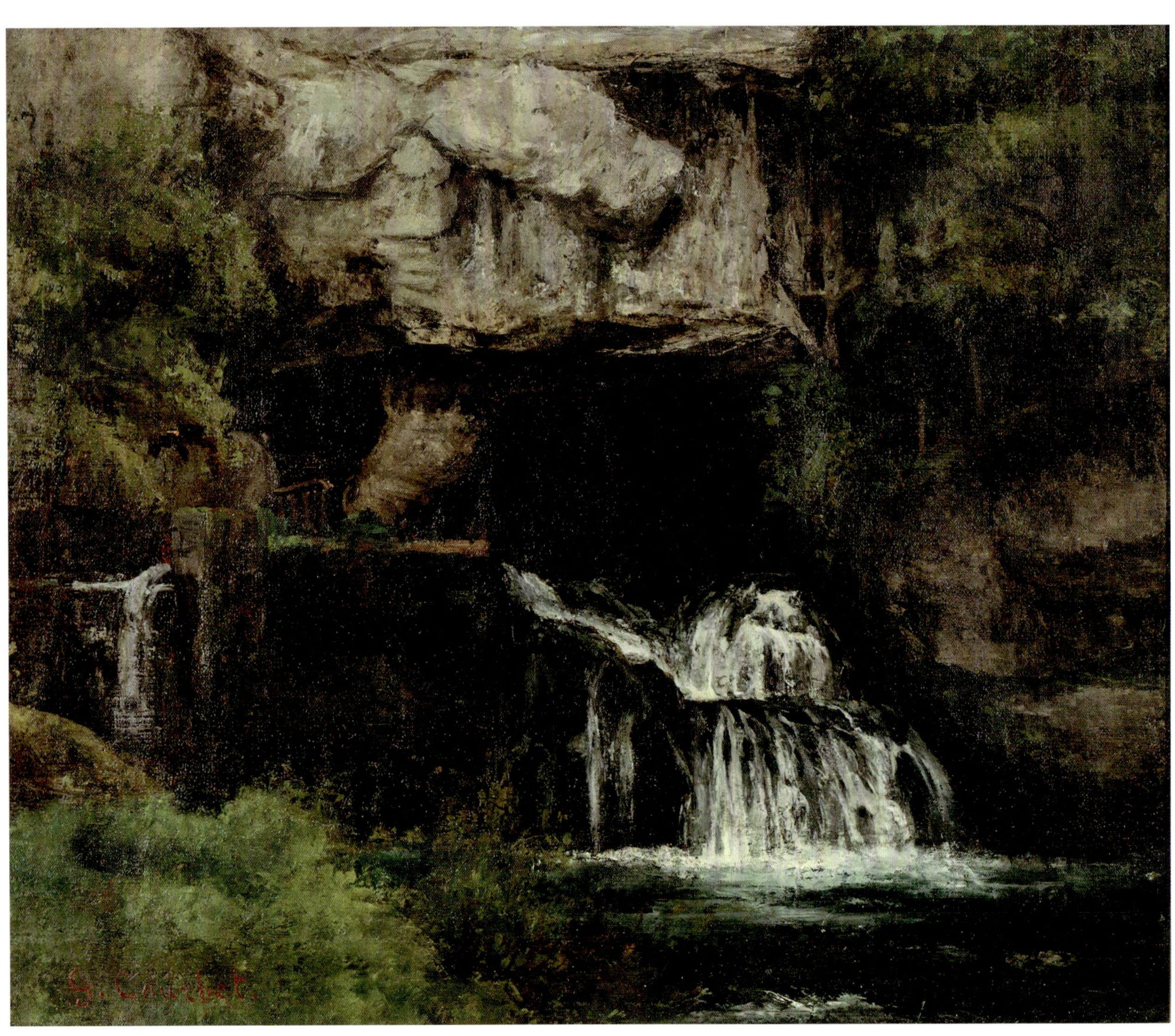

INTRODUCTION

ANDRÉ DOMBROWSKI

Gustave Courbet's 1860s grotto landscapes occupy a special place in the history of art. Dark and densely worked, they forestall visual entry and entangle the viewer near caves and undergrowth, obscuring any horizon that might allow escape. Often organized around dark holes from which rivers gush into opaque pools of water, with rock formations towering above, the paintings confine the viewer within remote worlds where the origins of streams emerge from underground. This dense, unsettling subterranean art was a major contribution to the history of modern landscape painting. Eschewing the omniscient, ruminative gaze typical of the landscape tradition, with its focus on deep vistas and roads leading into the distance (and thus a potentially redemptive future), Courbet instead often trapped viewers in a more immediate, close-up, and direct encounter with the real. Holding their gaze, he worked to forge an equivalence between the substances of the world—flowing water, moist rocks, lush greenery—and the viscosity of paint, intimately fusing theme and form. These landscapes were important for Paul Cézanne, the Impressionists, and subsequent modernist painters precisely for the perfect equilibrium they struck between the material and phenomenal presence of the depicted scenery and the newly acknowledged materials and painterly performances of representation.

The University of Pennsylvania recently realized that it has owned, since 1912, an important example of the genre (**FIG. 1.1**). The work came through the bequest of Thomas W. Evans,

FIG. 1.1 Gustave Courbet, *The Source of the Lison*, 1864, oil on canvas, 18 ½ × 22 in. (46 × 55 cm). University of Pennsylvania Art Collection, Gift of Thomas W. Evans, 1912.0005.0237.

dentist to the late nineteenth-century European courts and early benefactor of the university's school of dental medicine, whose late-1890s collection inventory records the painting. After not recognizing the canvas's import for over a hundred years, the university has now comprehensively studied, restored, and newly framed the work. Officially authenticated recently as well, it will be included for the first time in the next iteration of the Courbet catalogue raisonné.

The painting is a small but powerful example of Courbet's talent as a landscapist. It shows the source of the Lison River, in the painter's home region of the Franche-Comté, a site Courbet is known to have painted repeatedly around 1864. He would begin his drawing and painting on location, then finish the works in the studio. Less famous than his large-scale views of the nearby source of the river Loue (see fig. 7.2), of which we have more versions, only two other consistently authenticated paintings of the Lison have survived, making it a rarer subject for the painter and rendering the work's rediscovery all the more significant.[1] The largest among those previously known versions is dated 1864, held today in a private collection but on display at the Minnesota Marine Art Museum in Winona (it has generously been lent to the present exhibition for detailed comparison; **FIG. 1.2**). The Minnesota painting is larger than the Penn example, more of an exhibition picture. The other, smaller version, in an Italian private collection—along with one in Berlin's Alte Nationalgalerie whose authorship and subject are at times disputed (**FIG. 1.3**)—represents the sort of related paintings Courbet often made for the private market. The three more modest paintings are not copies of the Minnesota work but reimaginations of the same site, either started there as well or made entirely from the larger painting at a later date. The large canvas has an unusual vertical format, whereas the Penn canvas crops the site horizontally, showing more of the rock formations and greenery at the right and left of the source. While some of the foliage in the Minnesota painting is turning an autumnal brown, the greens are lusher in the Penn work, where the stream

FIG. 1.2 Gustave Courbet, *The Source of the Lison*, 1864, oil on canvas, 35 ⅞ × 28 ¾ in. (91.1 × 73 cm). Private Collection, Minnesota Marine Art Museum, Winona, Minnesota.

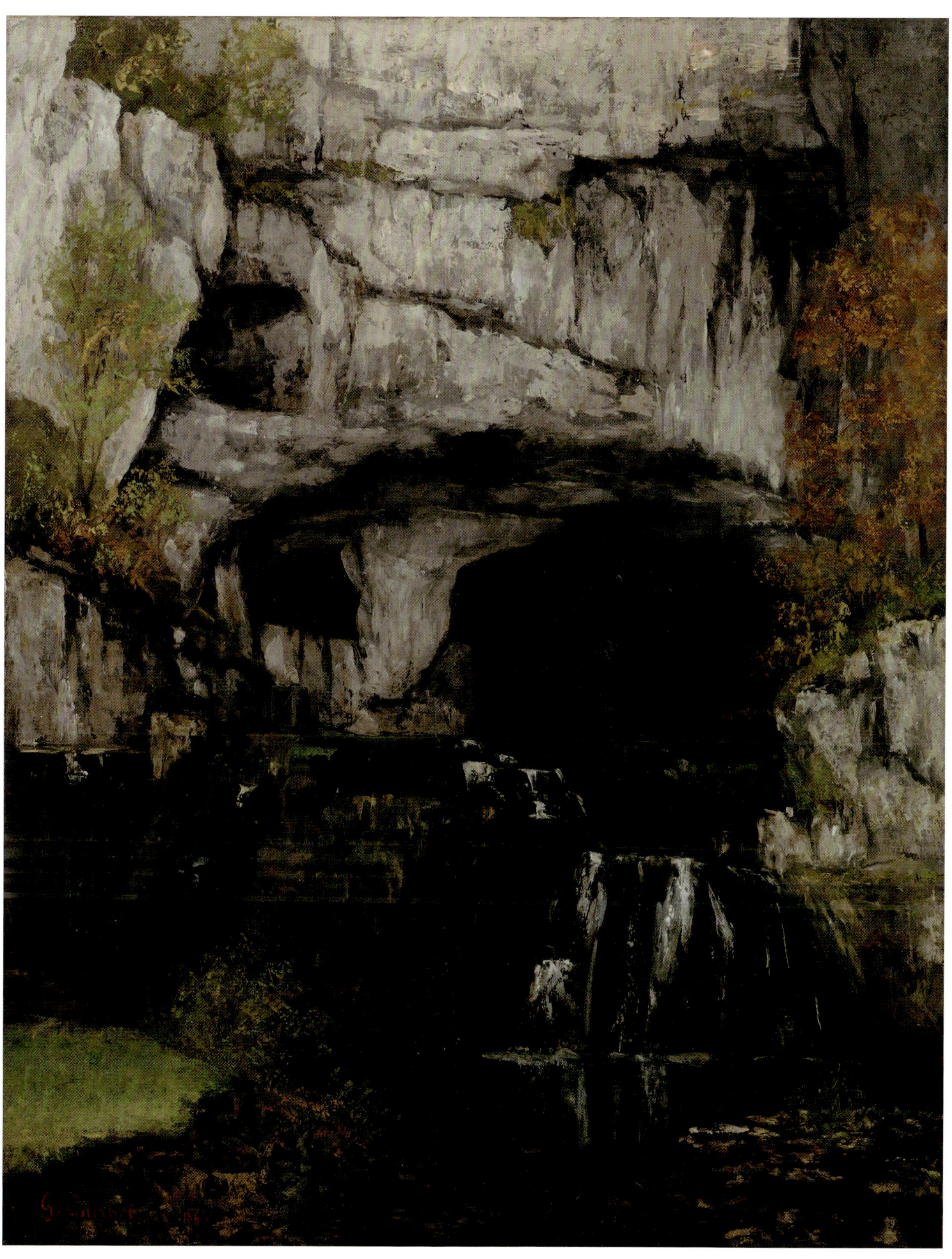

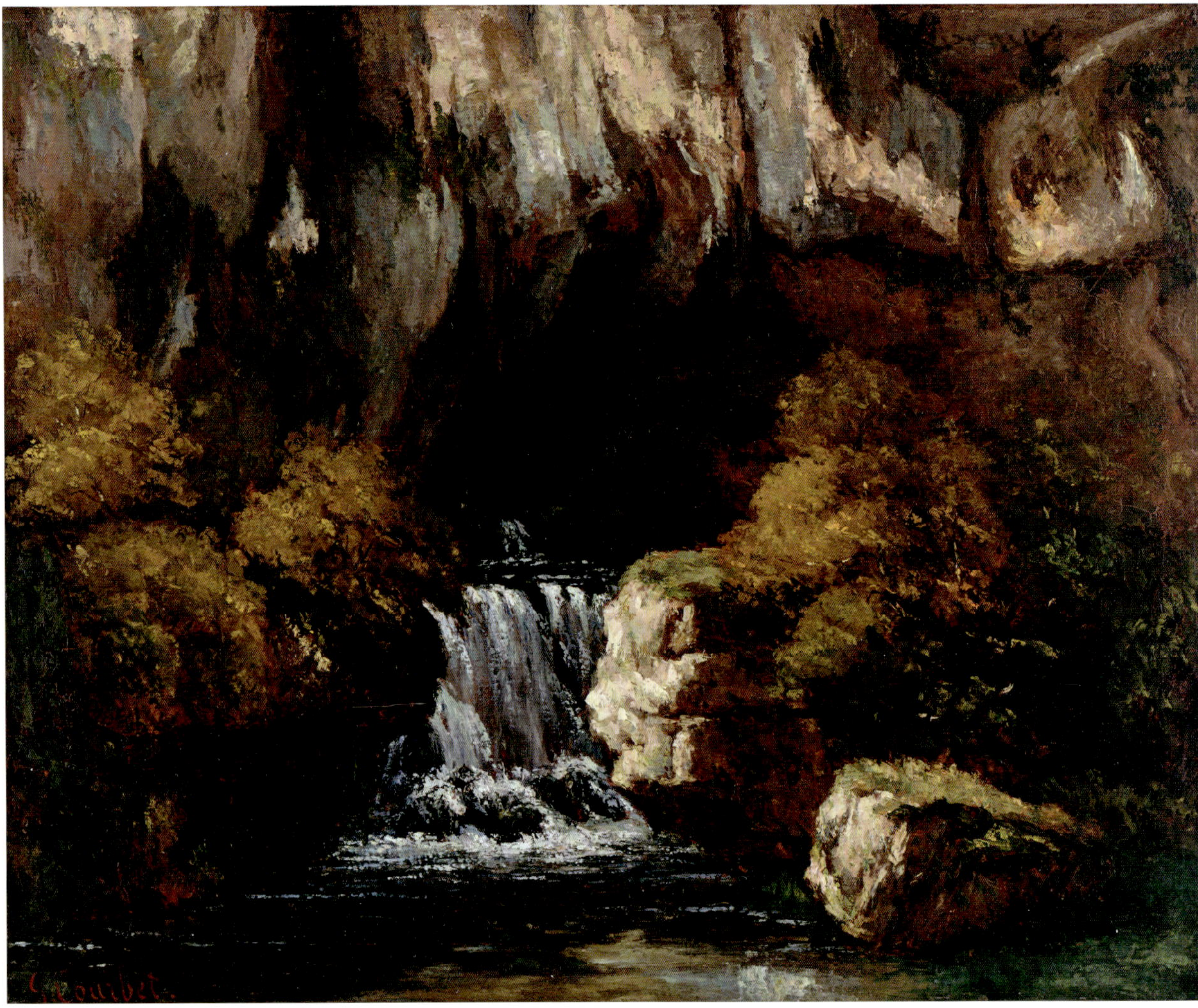

flows more heavily. Given the seasonal changes to the "ecosystem" in these paintings, Courbet also found subtly different ways to paint the water, leaves, and rocks.

The Penn canvas is devoid of figures, as are more or less all of Courbet's grotto paintings, but there is a subtle human presence. On the left of the scene, more visible in the Penn version than the Minnesota one, are a wooden staircase and platform erected at the site earlier in the century for visitors to the cave. The source of the Lison was surely a remote location, but it was not inaccessible. Courbet thoughtfully staged this scene of geological wonder, emphasizing the natural rock column that fans out at the top, seemingly holding open the mouth of the cave. To its right, at center, lies the darkest area of the canvas, with minimal

FIG. 1.3 Gustave Courbet? [attribution and subject disputed], *Source of the Lison*, ca. 1864, oil on canvas, 25 ¹³⁄₁₆ × 31 ¹¹⁄₁₆ in. (65.5 × 80.5 cm). Nationalgalerie / Staatliche Museen, Berlin, NG 11/69.

painted detail, a gaping absence that both attracts and repels the
viewer. It is a pleasure to imagine how actively Courbet labored
to bring to life the experience of a visit to the secluded, mysterious
site, how intent he was to draw us into a world that is both
the origin of a stream and the very material depth of his
painterly practice.

The emergence of a painting of this kind allows a university
institution like Penn's Arthur Ross Gallery to examine the work
from a variety of scholarly angles, and the exhibition *At the
Source: A Courbet Landscape Rediscovered* and this accompanying
catalogue do just that. Several of the region's most prominent
Courbet scholars offer diverse ways of interpreting the scene,
highlighting the import of the discovery of the Penn canvas
for Courbet studies at large. These inquiries range from the
modernity of the painting's form and material presence, to its place
within the modern French landscape tradition, to its innovative
spectatorial engagement. On a thematic level, the essays in this
volume investigate the meaning of the site: an important locale
in the Franche-Comté imagination, the source of the Lison was
a place of both nascent tourism and scientific inquiry. Courbet
knew many of the regional geologists and other scholars of local
history, language, and culture, and his Source paintings capture a
specific nineteenth-century fascination with the earliest histories
of geological formation in the area where the painter grew up.
(We know, for instance, that the writer and regional activist
Max Buchon owned a version of *The Source of the Lison*, though
which one is not known.) The approaches to the painting in this
volume exemplify current academic trends in the environmental
humanities, deepening our appreciation for an early and
mid-nineteenth-century culture aware of changing ecosystems
and open to an emerging preservationist mindset.

The painting raises other issues as well. Given how frequently
Courbet painted the female figure, sometimes outdoors, and
given the overall anthropomorphic tendencies of the landscape
tradition, Courbet's grotto paintings have often been probed for
their gendered connotations. Executed in close chronological

proximity to the major "source" paintings, Courbet's *Origin of the World* (*L'Origine du monde*, see fig. 7.3)—a close-up view of female genitalia framed by thighs, a heap of pubic hair, drapes, and the lower torso—particularly begs the comparison. *The Source of the Lison* is therefore also a figment of the nineteenth-century male artistic imagination, a sexual fantasy that maps the female body onto a remote landscape.

The Arthur Ross Gallery's *At the Source* is augmented with a select group of loans of other Courbet landscapes and a few period publications about the region, which illuminate the artist's special engagement with the site. A detailed conservation report brings to light some of the technical features of the making of the museum's Lison painting. Of course, not all questions can be answered, perhaps especially why the painting had remained on campus since the 1912 bequest yet was not recognized for what it is for more than a century. Its early provenance is also unclear, and no record of this version seems to exist before the painting was listed in Evans's inventory, drafted upon his death. We do not know how or when he acquired the painting, for instance, only that it hung prominently in his Parisian home. By contrast, much is known about Courbet's innovative exhibition programs and strategic approach to the Paris Salon—information we can use to think more about how Courbet imagined his overall market and the role of the various Lison versions and their differing formats.

Courbet's landscapes have not always been a favorite with art historians, who have often preferred his more politically biting figural work. It did not help that after the Paris Commune of 1871, when Courbet was charged with repaying the cost of rebuilding the Vendôme Column he had helped bring down during the civil unrest, and during his subsequent exile to Switzerland in 1873, a small industry of Courbet landscapes emerged, few fully by his hand. A grotto landscape like *The Source of the Lison*, a site Courbet painted only in the mid-1860s, can be ascribed more firmly to his hand, but questions about later revisions and restorations never quite go away. Courbet's oeuvre thus always beckons consideration of originality and coauthorship—issues that were less settled in the nineteenth-century context than they have been made to appear in modernist art practice and history, with its hero worship of the singular artist.

All these issues, and more, are broached in the following pages, and on the walls of the exhibition, and we hope that raising them will be an interesting exercise in bringing the complexity of both nineteenth-century French art history and institutional history to the broader public. The painting certainly warrants being dusted off and receiving close examination after so many years in obscurity.

1. For a more detailed account of various versions of Courbet's *Source of the Lison*, see Petra ten-Doesschate Chu's essay in this volume, "Courbet and the Source of the Lison: Geological Curiosity, Industrial Power Source, and 'Natural Site of an Artistic Character,'" 30n2.

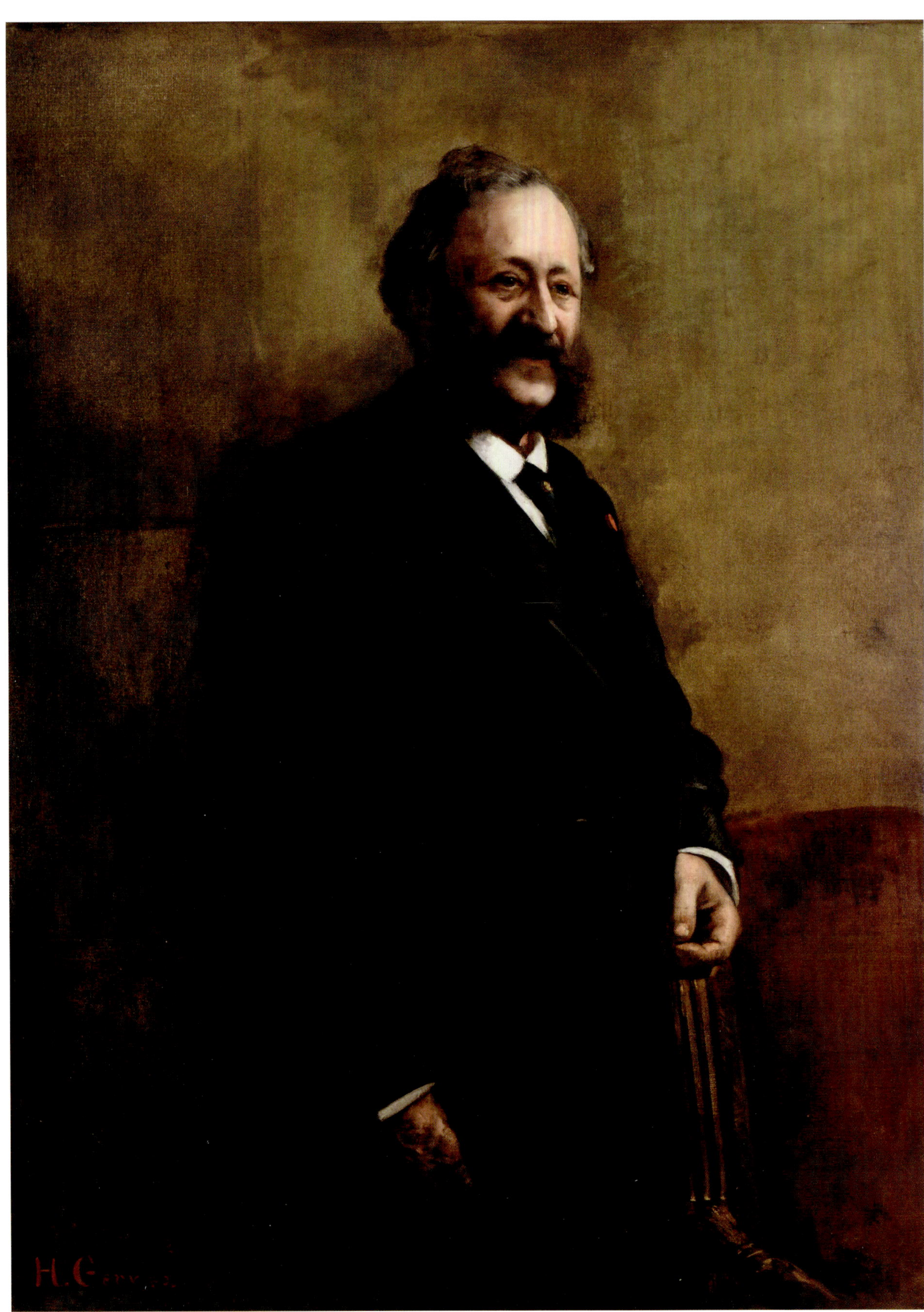

THOMAS W. EVANS:

A Gilded Life and Legacy

LYNN MARSDEN-ATLASS

Bella Rosa, the mid-nineteenth-century home of Philadelphia-born Dr. Thomas W. Evans (**FIG. 2.1**) and his wife, Agnes J. Evans, was located at 43, avenue Bois de Boulogne in the new sixteenth arrondissement in Paris. Surrounded by gardens and fields, the residence was bounded on one side by the grand tree-lined avenue de l'Impératrice (now avenue Foch) that led east to the Place de l'Étoile and to the west to the Bois de Boulogne.

Beginning in 1853, Emperor Napoléon III and Baron Georges-Eugène Haussmann launched a series of public works projects to improve the traffic, sanitation, and water supply for the booming metropolis. Haussmann managed to rebuild the city of Paris in just seventeen years, creating eighty kilometers of broad, tree-lined boulevards with expansive vistas. In 1852, Napoléon III had ceded the land to the city of Paris to create the Bois de Boulogne, a 2,088-acre public park on the western edge of the city whose picturesque landscapes included two lakes, a waterfall, a hippodrome, stables, the Pré Catelan pavilion, restaurants, cafés, and a zoo. Napoléon III was personally involved in the design of the park, which aspired to rival Hyde Park in London. One of the wonders of the new park was La Grande Cascade (**FIG. 2.2**), an artificial landscape constructed in 1856 from massive sandstone blocks brought from Fontainebleau. Its rocky facade, whose summit is a deep grotto from which a spring bubbles forth to a twenty-four-foot waterfall, replicates the sublime natural wonders of Gustave Courbet's native Jura

FIG. 2.1 Henri Gervex, *Thomas W. Evans*, 1892, oil on canvas, 45 × 34 in. (114.3 × 86.36 cm). University of Pennsylvania Art Collection, Gift of Dr. Thomas W. Evans, 1912.0005.0163.

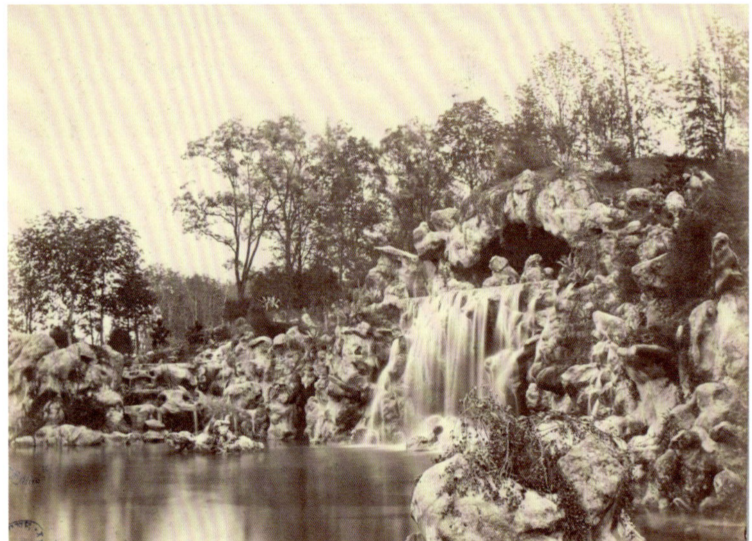

region, which the artist depicted in his source of the Lison landscapes of the 1860s (see figs. 1.1, 1.2). La Grande Cascade quickly became the favored meeting place in the Bois de Bologne, and by 1857, the Pavillon de la Grande Cascade offered fine dining in this romantic setting.

How did a young man from West Philadelphia find himself living in this grand location? Thomas W. Evans first established himself in Paris in 1847, joining the dental practice of a fellow American, Cyrus Brewster. In July 1850, Evans was called upon to treat Napoléon III for a terrible toothache. A mutual respect developed, and Evans became a frequent visitor to the palace and surgeon dentist to Napoléon III and the Empress Eugénie. When the emperor sent Evans to provide dental care to other European royalty, he doubled as a diplomatic emissary. Privy to discussions and plans for the expansion of Paris with Napoléon III and Baron Haussmann, Evans made strategic land investments, and by 1867 he was astonishingly wealthy.

In 1857–58, Evans purchased the farmland to construct a *hôtel* (which in the nineteenth century signified a home with aristocratic pretensions) in the architectural style of the Second Empire (**FIG. 2.3**). The property featured a carriage entrance, extensive stables with stalls for twenty horses, a greenhouse, a fountain and jet, an aviary, and beds of roses everywhere.

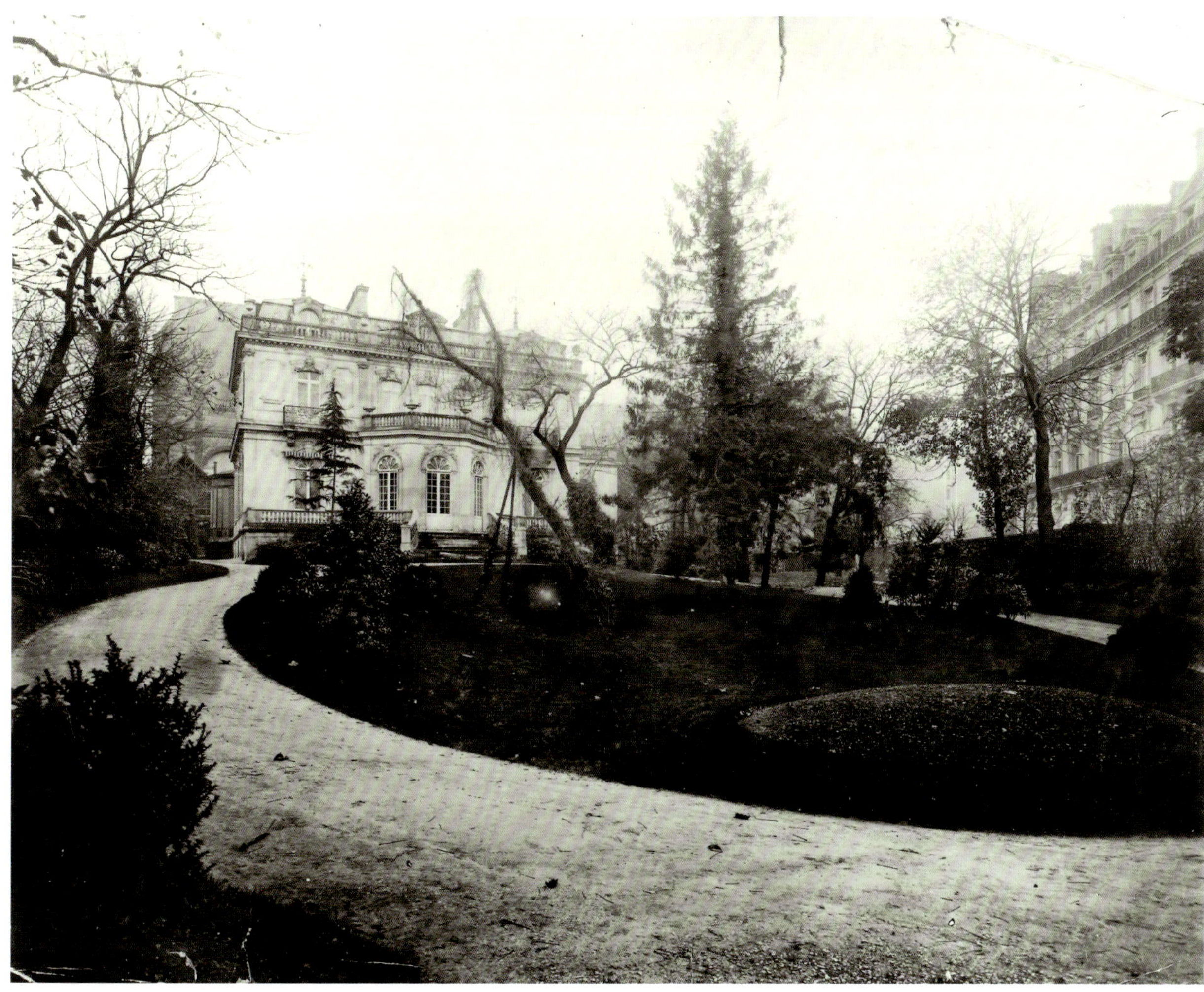

Bella Rosa was also the first home in Paris to have central heating, American-style plumbing, and underground heating for its gardens and aviary.

Bella Rosa comprised six rooms on each floor, with a marble stairway, a library, a gallery for Evans's paintings, and a white and gold ballroom. Stained-glass windows cast a jeweled light on Sèvres vases, rare tapestries and carpets, gifts from Europe's nobility, and a display of decorations and bibelots received from royal patients. While Evans's art collecting began with representations of Niagara Falls, cows, and sunrises, his collection of paintings improved in quality as his taste became more cultivated over time.[1]

Evans's collection of paintings, with a few exceptions, reflected the conventional taste of the Second Empire. Some of these paintings were acquisitions from the annual Salon, while others were contemporary French works. Still others were gifts from royalty, such as a portrait of the doctor's dog, Mitzy, a gift from the Queen of Belgium. In certain instances, Evans's choice of landscape and genre paintings may have been inspired by works in the Empress Eugénie's collection, twenty-one of which were first exhibited to the public at the Paris Exposition Universelle of 1867.[2] Among her landscapes in the exhibition were Charles-François Daubigny's *The Wide Valley at Optevoz* (*La Grande vallée d'Optevoz*; 1857, Château de Compiègne) and Courbet's *The Death of the Deer* (*L'Hallali du cerf*; 1867, Musée d'Orsay, Paris). The latter was one of two Courbet paintings Eugénie owned, as she acquired *Covered Brook* (*Le Ruisseau couvert*; n.d., Musée d'Orsay) at an unknown date.[3] The Empress also loaned a commissioned work by Rosa Bonheur, *Sheep at the Bank of the Sea* (*Moutons au bord de la mer*; 1864, National Museum of Women in the Arts, Washington, DC). As regent, Eugénie bestowed the Legion of Honor (Chevalier d'honneur) on Bonheur on June 8, 1865, making her the first female artist ever to receive it.

Notably, these three artists, Bonheur, Courbet, and Daubigny, were listed in the January 1898 inventory of Evans's estate (**FIGS. 2.4-6**).[4] Hanging in the large picture gallery (according to the inventory) were landscapes by Belgian, Dutch, French, German, and Swiss artists. They included "a picture signed Corot, landscape with marsh in the foreground, valued at sixty francs; a picture, portrait of Doctor Evans, by Gervex, and a picture, signed Courbet, water fall in the mountain, valued at seventy francs."[5] In a small room at one side of the office was "a work in crayon, black and white by Rosa Bonheur, 1863, 'A Cow' valued at one hundred fifty francs."[6]

At the 1867 Exposition Universelle in Paris, Evans and his fellow American Gardner Colton introduced nitrous oxide for use as general anesthesia to the European medical and dental communities. The use of this anesthesia, along with his innovative dentistry employing gold-foil fillings and vulcanite dentures, made Evans the dentist of European royalty from Britain to

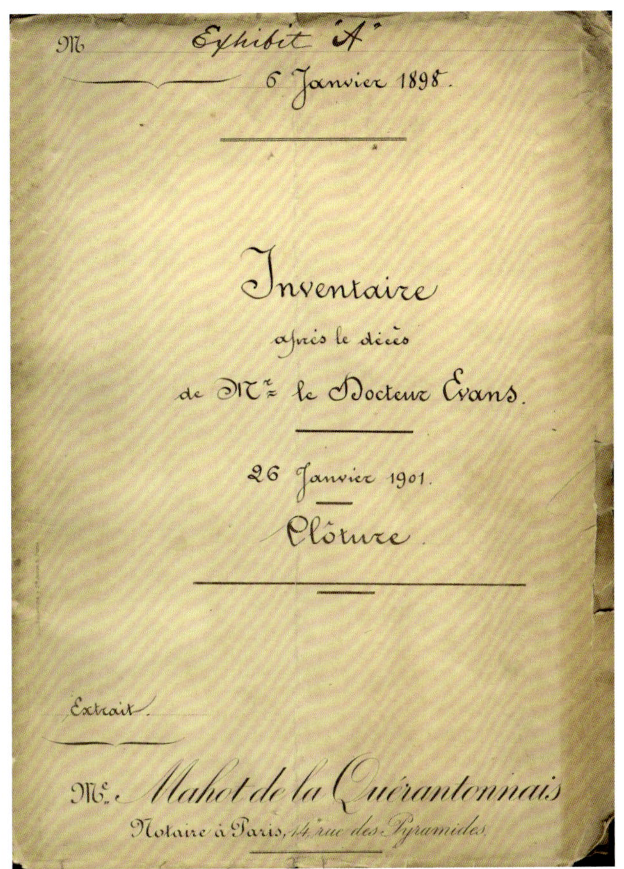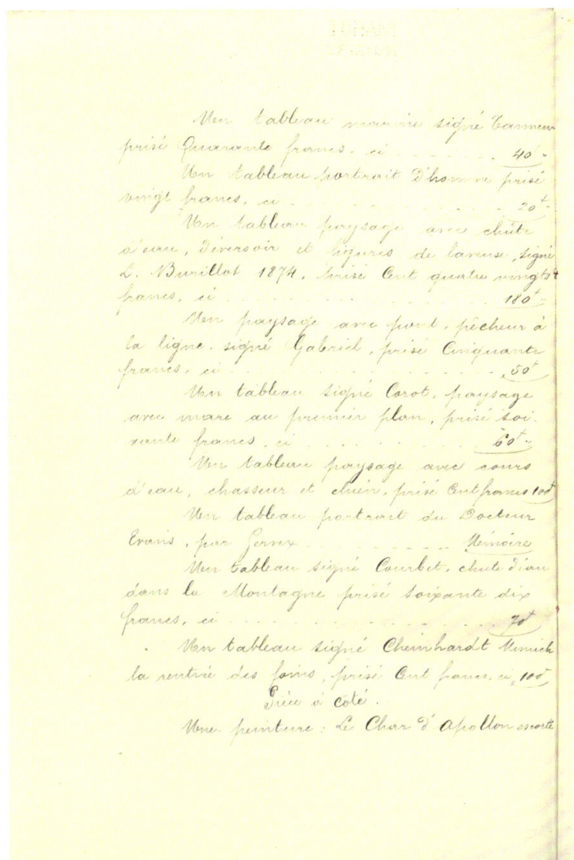

FIGS. 2.4–6 "Exhibit 'A' 6 Janvier 1898," from "Inventaire après le décès de M. le Docteur Evans," handwritten inventory on paper. Kislak Center for Special Collections, Rare Books and Manuscripts, University of Pennsylvania, Joseph W. Catharine Papers regarding the Thomas W. Evans Estate.

Russia and as far away as Turkey. Awarded the Legion of Honor by Napoléon III, Evans also played important roles in French and American politics. In 1870, as the Second Empire crumbled, Evans's decisive role in rescuing the Empress Eugénie in a daring escape to England made him a man of history. As chronicled in print and memorialized in Henri-Louis Dupray's 1884 painting *Departure of Empress Eugénie (Départ incognito)* (**FIG. 2.7**), Evans assisted the Empress to his waiting carriage as they commenced their escape at dawn.

In 1867, Evans also met the young actress Méry Laurent, who became his mistress for more than thirty years. Laurent was

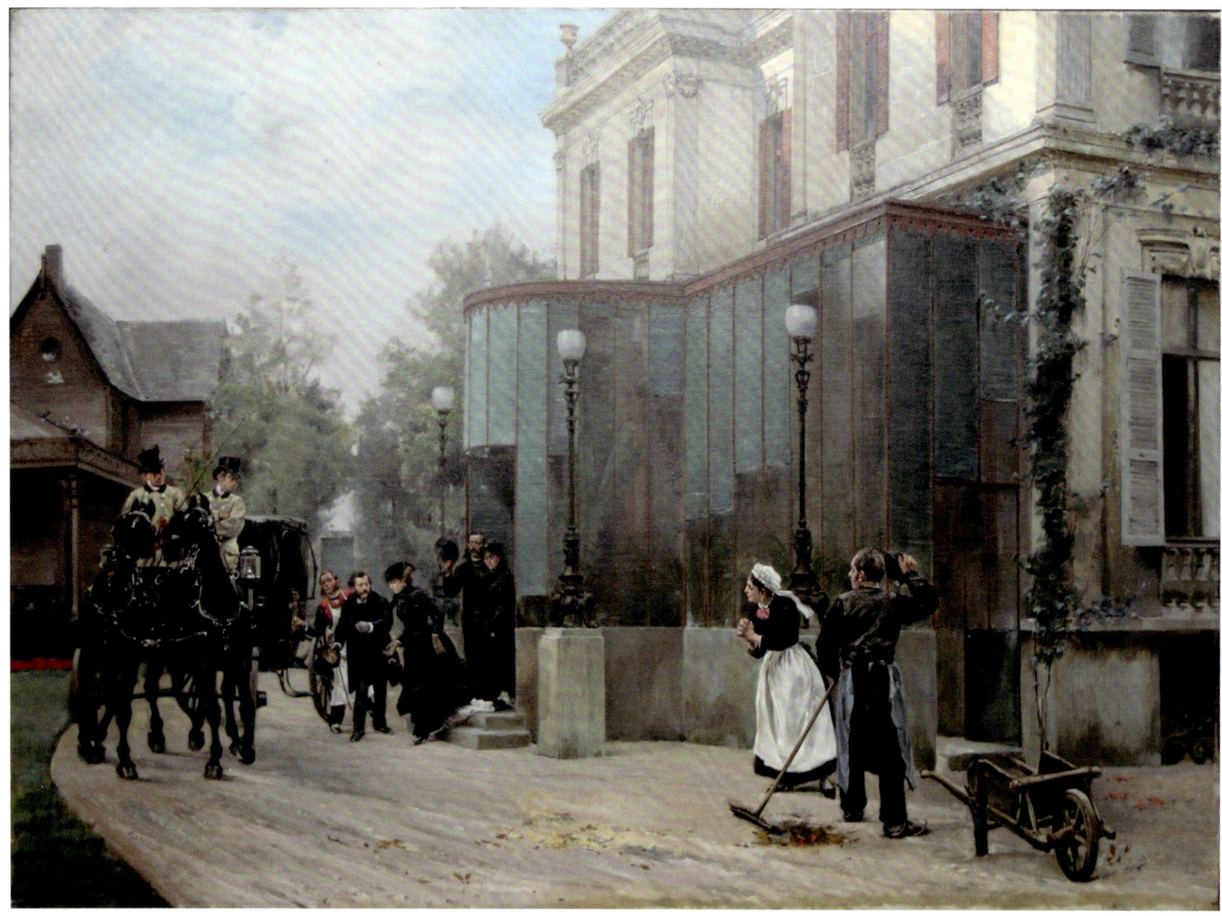

a favorite model of Edouard Manet and muse of Symbolist poet Stéphane Mallarmé. She introduced Evans to her circle of artists and writers and encouraged the dentist to acquire two oils and a watercolor by Manet, which were his most avant-garde acquisitions. These works are also recorded in the 1898 inventory as "an oil painting under glass by Manet 'Flowers in a Vase,' valued at a hundred fifty francs, 'Bun in a Delft Dish,' valued at one hundred fifty francs, and a water color by Manet, 'The Violin Player,' valued at one hundred francs."[7]

Evans became a publisher in 1868 when he founded the *American Register*, the first American weekly in Paris. In his later years, Evans established the Lafayette Home for Girls, a nonprofit residence for young American women who came to Paris to study art. His extraordinary life abruptly ended when Evans died of a heart attack at Bella Rosa on November 15, 1897.

FIG. 2.7 Henri-Louis Dupray, *Departure of Empress Eugénie (Départ incognito)*, 1884, oil on canvas, 23 × 28 ½ in. (58.4 × 72.4 cm). University of Pennsylvania Art Collection, Gift of Dr. Thomas W. Evans, 1912.0005.0057.

Since Thomas and Agnes Evans had no children, his extended family anticipated inheriting his great wealth. However, while Evans was generous to many, the bulk of his $5 million estate was to be used to establish the Thomas W. Evans Museum and Institute Society, whose charge was approved in the Court of Common Pleas No. 4 for the County of Philadelphia in 1897. The society's purpose was "the establishment, support and maintenance of a museum and dental institute in the City of Philadelphia in accordance with the Will of Dr. Thomas W. Evans . . . to erect suitable buildings to be called 'The Thomas W. Evans Museum & Dental Institute.'"[8] The will was contested by the family and remained unresolved in the French courts for several years.

On June 15, 1912, an agreement was signed between the Thomas W. Evans Museum and Institute Society and the Trustees of the University of Pennsylvania to erect the building on the site of the Evans Family Homestead at Fortieth and Spruce Streets in West Philadelphia. The Thomas W. Evans Museum and Dental Institute was dedicated on February 22–23, 1915, and the event was hailed as the greatest in dental history. From 1915 to 1967, the Evans Museum housed paintings, sculptures, jewelry, photographs, furniture, decorative arts, and Evans's renowned carriage (**FIG. 2.8**). In the spring of 1967, the museum was closed and the collection placed in storage to make way for a dental clinic. Thomas Evans's will was broken in Orphan's Court, and Dean D. Walter Cohen arranged to auction over two hundred items—paintings, sculptures, furniture, silver, jewelry, and decorative objects—from the Evans collection at Christie's (New York) in October 1983 for the benefit of the endowment of the Dental School.[9]

In January 2010, Denis Kinane, then dean of the University of Pennsylvania School of Dental Medicine, discovered a cache of unsold artworks from the Evans collection in offsite storage. Kinane asked me, in my role as university curator, to return these artifacts to campus. Thus began a lengthy process of identification and digitization. Over the next five years, these artworks were

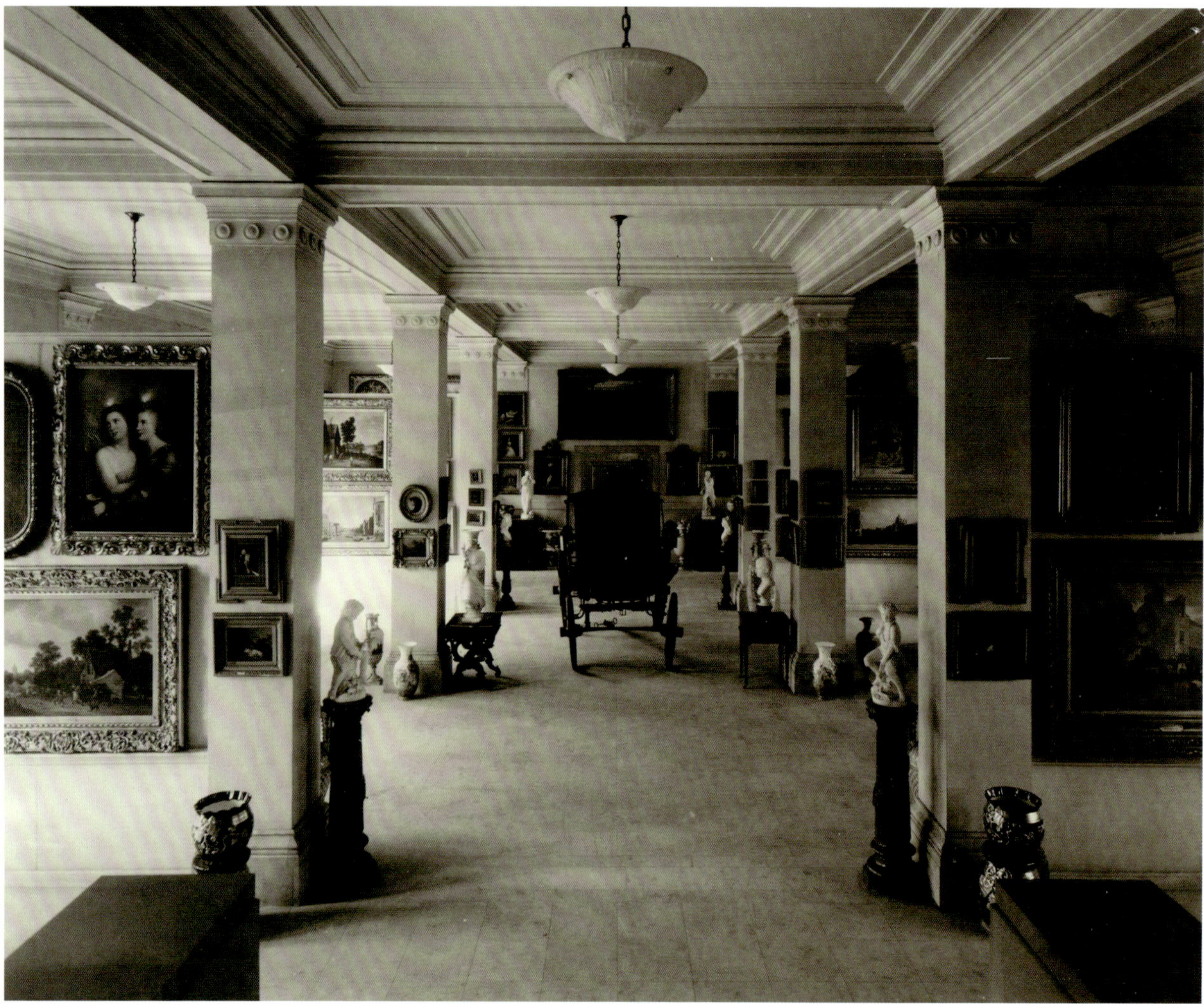

researched by scholars and restored to their original brilliance
by conservators.

The public unveiling of these superb artifacts was celebrated
in an exhibition at the Arthur Ross Gallery. *Courtly Treasures:
The Collection of Thomas W. Evans, Surgeon Dentist to Napoléon III*
(July 1–November 8, 2015) featured 130 paintings, sculptures,
photographs, furniture, and decorative arts drawn from the
Thomas W. Evans collection. The accompanying catalogue
offered new scholarship on the collection. The timing was
fortuitous: the show opened as the kickoff to the Centennial
of the Thomas W. Evans Museum and Dental Institute. At one
hundred, the historic Evans building needed updating, and
renovations of the building began in 2016. My phone rang one

FIG. 2.8 Photographer unknown, Thomas W.
Evans Museum, n.d. School of Dental Medicine,
Dental School Library Historical Collection
1798–1988, University Archives and Records
Center, University of Pennsylvania.

day that summer, and Elizabeth Ketterlinus, senior associate dean, Development & Alumni Relations, Penn Dental Medicine, announced that construction workers had located two boxes in the basement that might be of interest. An hour later, I was perusing their contents. Of interest were two hundred cartes de visite of European royalty and clients of Evans, a Nadar photograph of an unidentified woman, and an unframed canvas whose subject was obscured by darkened varnish. Three red letters—"G. Co"—in the signature held my interest, and I set the work aside. Having previously taught nineteenth-century French art in the museums in Paris, I suddenly realized I had seen this signature before.

We sent the painting to conservator Barbara Ventresco a few weeks later. Her post-conservation report reveals a close-cropped image of a landscape with vertical limestone rocks, a grotto, and a waterfall. It also includes the signature: G. Courbet. In Robert Fernier's *La Vie et oeuvre de Gustave Courbet: Catalogue raisonné*, images of similar paintings were listed as *Source du Lison*, while others were identified as *La Grotte* or *La Source de la Loue*.[10]

In the fall of 2016, we then consulted with André Dombrowski, associate professor in the Department of the History of Art at Penn, and Joseph Rishel, then curator of European painting and sculpture before 1900 for the John G. Johnson Collection and the Rodin Museum at the Philadelphia Museum of Art, who recommended contacting the Institut Gustave Courbet in Ornans, France, to submit a request for the Comité Courbet to examine the canvas for authentication. Was it or was it not painted by Gustave Courbet?[11]

In 2018, the Office of the Curator engaged the fine art scientific analysts Jennifer L. Mass and Adam C. Finnefrock to sample and analyze the pigments and canvas. Their executive summary documents their findings:

> The work examined in this study is a landscape painting on canvas, presumably in oil, that is similar in composition to three works attributed to Gustave Courbet (1819–1877). . . .

Preliminary non-invasive elemental analysis was carried out to determine if the palette of the work was consistent with that used by Courbet during his career, which would mean, barring any restoration materials, that none of the pigments, paint additives or substrate materials should post-date 1877. Analysis of twelve selected areas of the painting did not identify the presence of any anachronistic materials in the work, meaning that pigments and other materials inferred in this study would have been available to artists working from the 1860s and continue to be available today.[12]

In October 2021, André Dombrowski and I convened three renowned Courbet scholars to examine the painting at Penn and to discuss the organization of a scholarly exhibition on Courbet's Source of the Lison paintings in 2023. Petra ten-Doesschate Chu, Paul Galvez, and Mary Morton were enthusiastic about the project and agreed to write essays for the exhibition catalogue. That fall, the Office of the Curator submitted a second request to the Comité Courbet and received written confirmation that the committee would examine Penn's painting in April 2022 in New York. On May 17, an email from Sébastien Fernier, secretary of the Institut Gustave Courbet, confirmed their decision: "It's a Courbet, congratulations!" The 2023 exhibition *At the Source: A Courbet Landscape Rediscovered* celebrates Courbet's *Source of the Lison* in the Penn Art Collection and its newly recognized place in the artist's oeuvre of the 1860s.

1. Gerald Carson, *The Dentist and the Empress: The Adventures of Dr. Tom Evans in Gas-Lit Paris* (Boston: Houghton Mifflin, 1983), 72–73.

2. Alison McQueen, *Empress Eugénie and the Arts: Politics and Visual Culture in the Nineteenth Century* (Surry, England: Ashgate, 2011), 189–90.

3. McQueen, *Empress Eugénie and the Arts*, 189 and 222–23, Courbet no. 174, cited as belonging to the empress and loaned from Saint-Cloud. As McQueen notes on 222–24, the sculptor and superintendent of the arts Émilien de Nieuwerkerke acted as an intermediary for this purchase. See also *Expositions des oeuvres de M. G. Courbet, Rond-Point de l'Alma, Champs-Elysées* (Paris, 1867), 6–7.

4. Me. Mahot de la Quarantonnais (14, rue des Pyramides, Paris), "Inventaire après le décès de M. le Docteur Evans," January 26, 1901, Closure, 17.

5. Quarantonnais, "Inventaire," 17.

6. Quarantonnais, 18.

7. Quarantonnais, 19 and 21. See André Dombrowski, "Dr. Evans's Manets," in *Courtly Treasurers: The Collection of Thomas W. Evans, Surgeon Dentist to Napoléon III*, Arthur Ross Gallery (Philadelphia: Arthur Ross Gallery, 2015), 59–67.

8. Court of Common Pleas No. 4 for the County of Philadelphia, December term, 1897, no. 1450.

9. For a complete account of the history of the Thomas W. Evans Museum and collection, see Arthur Ross Gallery, *Courtly Treasures*, 21–26.

10. See Robert Fernier, *La Vie et l'oeuvre de Gustave Courbet: Catalogue raisonné* (Lausanne: Bibliothèque des arts; Fondation Wildenstein, 1977–78).

11. See Petra ten-Doesschate Chu, "Courbet or Not Courbet, That Is the Question," *IFAR Journal* 7, no. 1 (2004): 18–26, reprinted in this volume, 81–96.

12. Jennifer L. Mass and Adam C. Finnefrock, Scientific Analysis of Fine Art, LLC, "Pigment Analysis of a Landscape on Canvas Attributed to Gustave Courbet," Scientific Analysis of Fine Art Report 1760, July 30, 2018, Philadelphia, Pennsylvania, partially reprinted in this volume, 105–7.

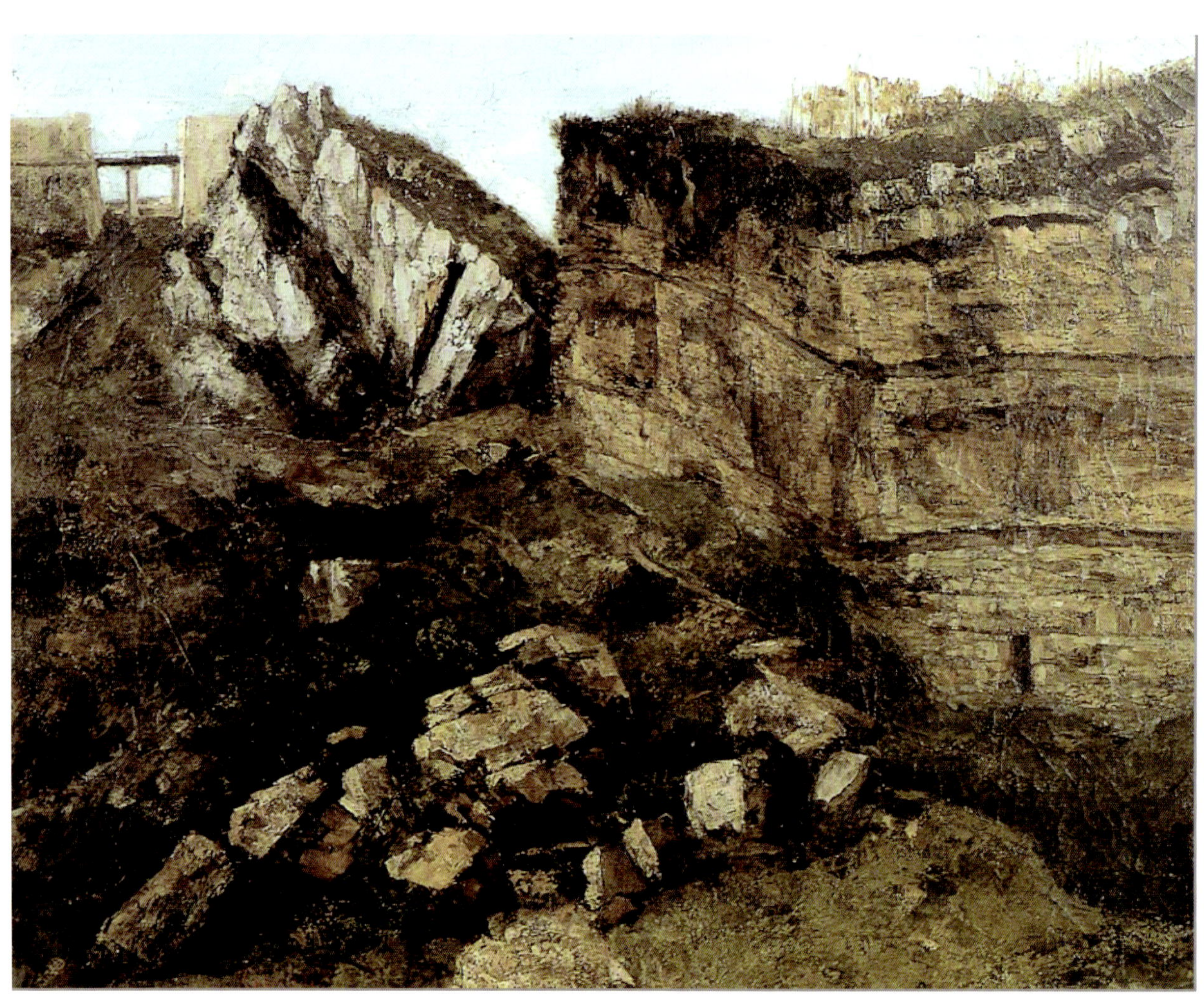

COURBET AND THE SOURCE OF THE LISON:

Geological Curiosity, Industrial Power Source, and "Natural Site of an Artistic Character"

PETRA TEN-DOESSCHATE CHU

Beginning in the fall of 1863, following the construction of a new, state-of-the-art studio in Ornans,[1] Gustave Courbet spent twenty months in his hometown, taking only local trips to visit friends. This prolonged stay, unusual for the peripatetic artist, led to the production of a group of major landscapes depicting spectacular natural sites in the Doubs and Jura departments of the Franche-Comté. Courbet's paintings of the spring of the Lison River, including the University of Pennsylvania's *The Source of the Lison* (*La Source du Lison*; see fig. 1.1), the subject of the present exhibition,[2] were part of this group of works that also included canvases depicting the source of the Loue River, the cliffs of Chauveroche, the Gour de Conche waterfall (see fig. 3.4), the rocky interior of the Saracen cave, and the clifftop Fort de Joux.[3] These paintings, most of them focused on geological wonders of Courbet's native Franche-Comté, reflect the admiration for the region's spectacular scenery he shared with fellow members of the rural bourgeoisie, as well as their interest in its natural and human history. They also hint at Courbet's awareness of the conflict that was arising, after the middle of the nineteenth century, between the agricultural and industrial exploitation of the region's resources—its forests, springs, and rocks—and the nascent movement to preserve and eventually restore their natural beauty.

FIG. 3.1 Gustave Courbet, *The Roche Pourrie: Geological Study*, 1864, oil on canvas, 23 ½ × 28 ¾ in. (59.7 × 73 cm). Musée Max-Claudet, F.409, courtesy of Musée des Beaux-Arts de Dole.

Courbet's lengthy stay in his native region in 1864 not only produced some of his most impressive landscape paintings but also led to the revival of old friendships and the forging of new ones. Like Courbet himself, his social circle in the Franche-Comté belonged to the rural bourgeoisie. This well-to-do landowning and industrial class owed its comfortable status to logging, agriculture, viticulture, cattle raising, salt mining, and iron ore extraction; and to related industries such as furniture making, rapeseed oil production, wine and cheese making, and the manufacture of metal wire and tools.[4] The area's many rivers drove numerous mills that provided power to local industry. In the mid-nineteenth century, the Doubs department alone boasted some 570 mills, used for grinding, sawing, pumping, and pounding.[5]

As in other regions of France, the interest of the rural bourgeoisie in the land on which they—and their ancestors before them—lived led to the formation of so-called *sociétés d'émulation* (emulation societies), regional associations that organized lectures on local history, archaeology, folklore, monumental heritage, geology, botany, entomology, and industry, and published their proceedings in *Mémoires*.[6] The three Franche-Comté departments (Haute-Saône, Jura, and Doubs) all had their own societies, founded, respectively, in 1801, 1817, and 1841. The membership rolls of these societies, regularly published in the *Mémoires*, included many in Courbet's social circle, both friends and patrons. The artist himself is listed as a member of the Société d'émulation du Doubs in 1853.[7]

Not surprisingly, given the Franche-Comté's spectacular geography, the members of the emulation societies showed deep interest in its physical origins. In the mid-nineteenth century, the historiography of the Jura's geological past was still young. Though its feeble beginnings dated to the eighteenth century, the geologist Jules Marcou, in his 1888 article "Les Géologues et la géologie du Jura jusqu'en 1870," rather self-servingly argued that its "truly creative period" had begun in the 1840s with his mentor

Claude-Marie Germain, a medical doctor and amateur geologist in his native Salins, and culminated in his own work.[8] Marcou did acknowledge the contribution of older geologists, in particular Alexandre Brongiart, one of the pioneers—together with William Smith in Britain—of biostratigraphy, the dating of rock strata by analyzing the specific fossils assembled within them. Indeed, it was Brongiart who had suggested that the limestone karst of the Jura mountains belonged to a distinct era of the Mesozoic period (between the Triassic and the Cretaceous), which he baptized "Jurassic."[9]

While not an active member of the Société d'émulation du Doubs, Courbet must have been aware of the major themes covered in the society's lectures and proceedings, themes that percolated in the local media and in discussions in homes and cafés. He doubtless knew that the Jura mountains in the Franche-Comté resulted from a folding of the earth's crust that comprised layers from different geological periods, all formed from the accumulation of faunal detritus of shallow seas. The skeletons of billions of sea creatures, small and large, had formed a water-soluble limestone (karst) in which rain had slowly hollowed out underground rivers, sinkholes, and caves. Courbet's acquaintance with Marcou in 1864, during a lengthy stay in Salins to visit the writer Max Buchon and the sculptor Max Claudet, must have increased his interest in and knowledge of the geological peculiarities of the region. Marcou, who had recently returned to his native Salins from a four-year sojourn in North America, presented Courbet with several Indigenous American weapons to decorate his new studio.[10] He also commissioned the artist to paint a "geological study" of the Roche pourrie (**FIG. 3.1**), a dramatic cliff just outside of Salins, so named because over time large pieces of rock had broken away from it and fallen down. Marcou had studied the fault intensely in his youth, finding numerous fossils of small marine creatures embedded in the layers of limestone. He had even lent his own name to one: *Hyboclypus Marcou*.[11] In his painting of the site, Courbet represents the geologist as a tiny figure among gigantic pieces of rock, leaning forward, perhaps to examine a fossil closely. One imagines him marveling at the thought of the Jurassic ocean in which this creature had lived its short life some two hundred million years ago.

THE SOURCE OF THE LISON

Courbet first painted the source of the Lison River in October 1864, while on his way from Ornans to Salins (see fig. 1.2). The site is one of several karst springs in the Franche-Comté, together with the source of the Loue River and Source Bleue (the spring of the Cusancin River), all painted by Courbet. His friend Claudet accompanied him to the Lison spring site and recorded the genesis of the painting.[12] He reports that it was completed in two hours, almost entirely with a palette knife. Courbet explained the use of the knife to Claudet as a way to emulate the natural processes that had led to the formation of the landscape: "Try a brush to do the rocks like that, rocks that have been eroded by the weather and the rain, which have formed long seams from top to bottom."[13] To Courbet, the erosive force of wind and rain could not be simulated with the soft hairs of a paintbrush; they required the hard metal of the blade.[14]

In his paintings of the spring, Courbet highlights the impressive grandeur of the Lison River, gushing out of the dark limestone cave and forming large cascading streams. Despite his deliberately close-up viewpoint, standing or seated at his easel in front of the source, he cannot have failed to see the mill buildings on one side. Taking a deep dive in the Doubs archives, Nathalie Vidal has found that the source of the Lison, which for centuries was privately owned, had been used to drive water mills since the Middle Ages. In 1830, it was acquired by the mayor of the nearby village Nans-sous-Sainte-Anne, Sébastien Crétin, whose son Frédéric planned a huge industrial establishment with numerous mills and factories meant to turn the village into a "grand industrial center."[15] Though it is not known exactly how much of Frédéric's grandiose plan materialized, a lithograph titled *The Source of the Lison River Seen from the*

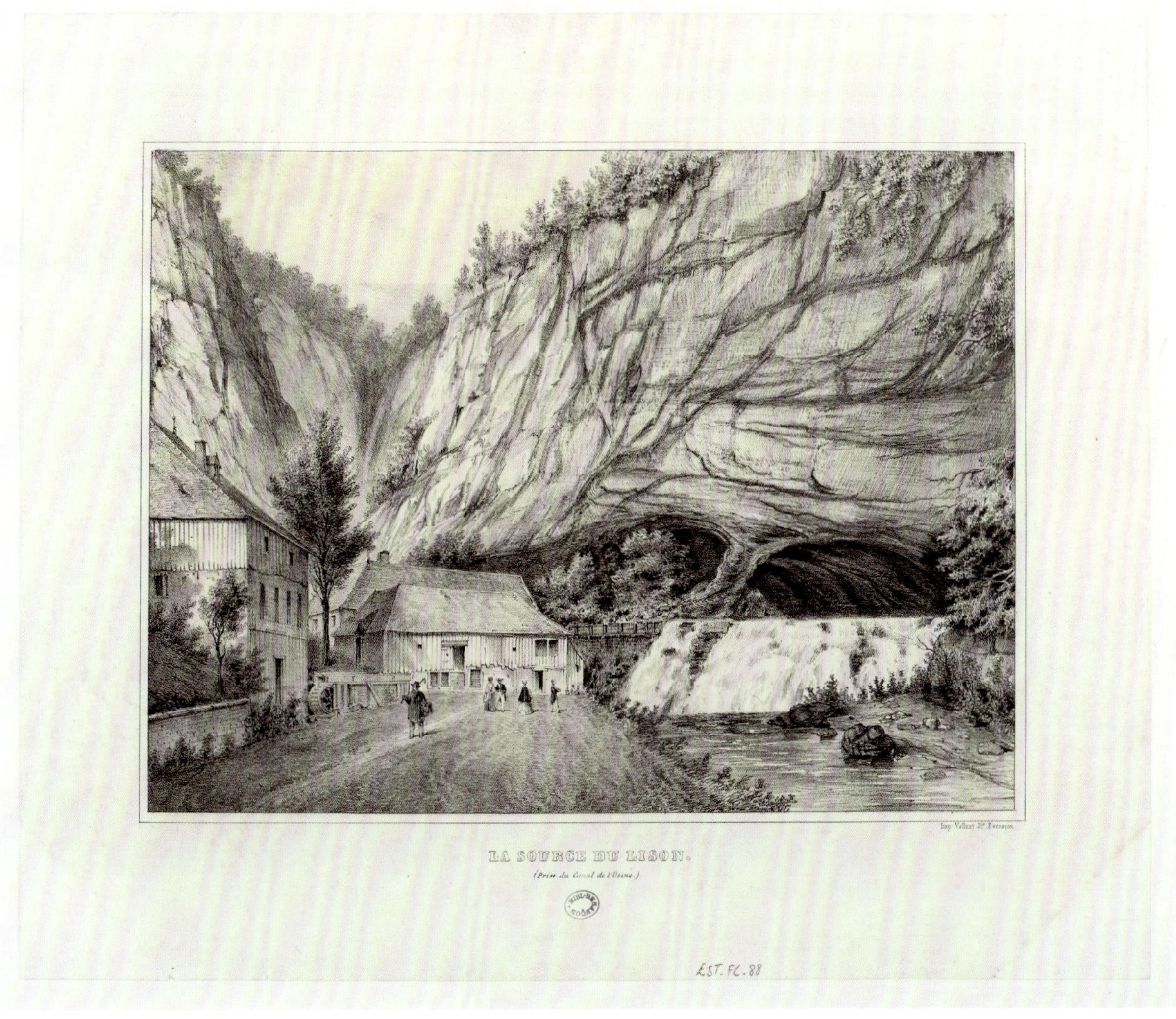

FIG. 3.2 Valluet Jeune, publisher, *The Source of the Lison River Seen from the Canal of the Factory*, 19th century, lithograph, 8 ⅟₁₆ × 11 in. (20.5 × 27.9 cm). Bibliothèque municipale de Besançon.

Factory Canal (*La Source du Lison prise du Canal de l'Usine*; FIG. 3.2), from the middle of the century, shows a group of buildings on the side of the source of the Lison connected by a bridge to a mill in one of the cascading streams.[16] An electricity plant, probably built by the Compagnie électrique Loue-Lison around 1910, is still visible on a postcard from the early twentieth century (FIG. 3.3).

Courbet's paintings of the source of the Lison exclude the human-made and unpicturesque aspects of the site, presenting the spring as an untouched natural landscape. Such nostalgic idealism, ostensibly compromising the realism in art promoted by Courbet, was characteristic of the artist's other landscapes paintings of 1864 as well.[17] Charles Toubin recounts that in his

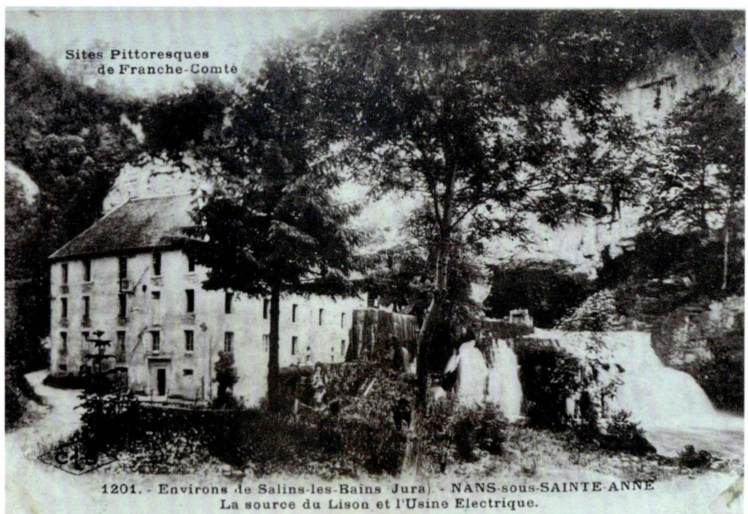

FIG. 3.3 "Sites Pittoresques de Franch-Comté: 1201. Environs de Salins-les-Bains (Jura). Nans-sous-Sainte-Anne. La Source du Lison et l'Usine Electrique," ca. 1900, postcard. Collection of Petra ten-Doesschate Chu.

painting of the Gour de Conche (**FIG. 3.4**), "Courbet gave the cascade more water than it had on the day it posed for him, he made that water whiter, [and] added foliage." When Toubin took him to task, Courbet answered, "It's nothing. A few beauty spots."[18] As in the case of the source of the Lison, Courbet obscured the effects of the region's agricultural and industrial development on the famed waterfall. By "adding" water, he glossed over the consequences wrought by the gradual depletion of rivers and streams through agricultural and industrial developments.[19] And by making the water whiter than it looked in reality, he disguised the evidence of aquatic pollution, resulting especially from the booming iron industry in the Franche-Comté region.[20]

COURBET AND CHARLES BEAUQUIER

Courbet's effort, especially in his landscapes of 1864, to erase human intervention in nature from his landscape paintings has a curious parallel in the contemporaneous writings of Charles Beauquier, a writer, journalist, and politician born in Besançon. Beauquier was a friend of Courbet (in his letters of the early 1870s, the artist addresses him as "Mon cher Beauquier"), but the details of their friendship have remained vague. While Courbet was painting his spectacular Franche-Comté "*paysages*

FIG. 3.4 Gustave Courbet, *The Fall of Gour de Conche, Myon*, 1864, oil on canvas, 29 ⅛ × 23 ⅝ in. (74 × 60 cm). Musée des Beaux-Arts et d'Archéologie, Besançon, D.953.1.3.

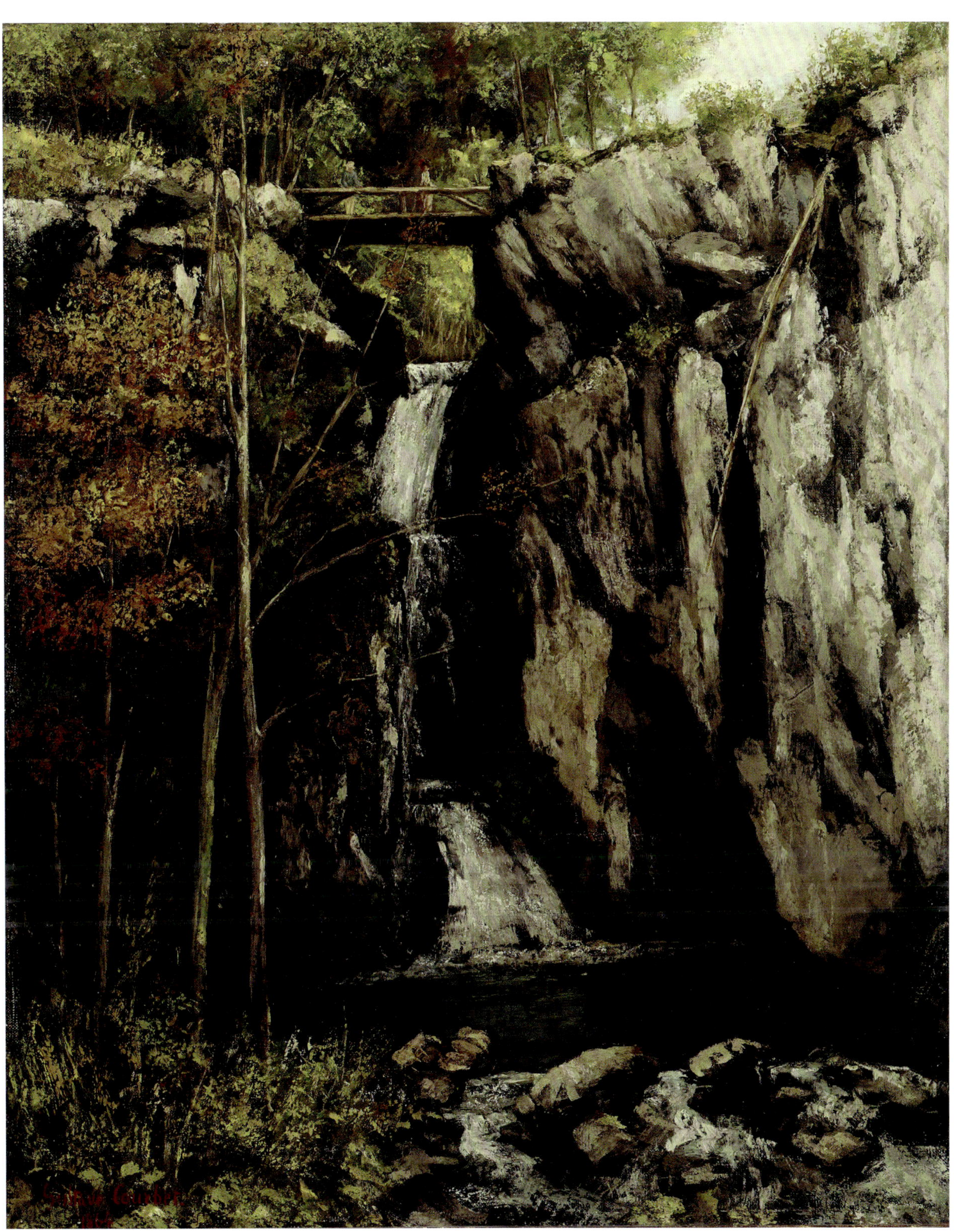

sauvages" (savage landscapes), as he described them in a letter to his dealer Jules Luquet,[21] Beauquier was writing a book, *Philosophie de la musique*, to be published in 1865. Beauquier's text argues that, just as instrumental (as opposed to vocal) music is the highest and preeminently "modern" form of music, landscape painting of undomesticated natural sites is the highest and preeminently modern form of painting.[22] Both, according to Beauquier, originated in Northern European Romanticism, a process that for painting he describes as follows: "One day, that entire apparatus of [human-made] structures, which seemed indispensable to the landscape, finally disappears, and nature bursts into the frame, pure, free nature, independent of human constructions, nature for its own sake, with its rocks, its fields, and vast horizons."[23]

We do not know whether Courbet, in 1864, was familiar with Beauquier's ideas, but there is a tantalizing link between the *paysages sauvages* he painted that year and Beauquier's lifelong efforts to preserve the undomesticated French landscape, culminating in 1906 in the so-called Beauquier Law. A political victory for Beauquier that was years in the making, the law concerned the practical organization of "the protection of natural sites and monuments of an artistic character."[24] It was the product of the author's deep love of the scenery of the Franche-Comté, such as the source of the Loue and the source of the Lison. Beauquier cited both in his initial proposal of the law in 1901, in which he deplored the "vulgar" industrial constructions that, like ugly growths, had come to disfigure these sites, spoiling the incomparable tableau that each one of them offered.[25]

Courbet died nearly thirty years before the adoption of the Beauquier Law and played no active role in the landscape-preservationist efforts of the late nineteenth century that had led to it. Nonetheless, it is tempting to think that his 1864 paintings of natural sites in the Franche-Comté, "cleansed" of the industrial structures and pollution that had diminished their aesthetic value, may have contributed to their preservation and restoration in the twentieth century. Using the language of present-day

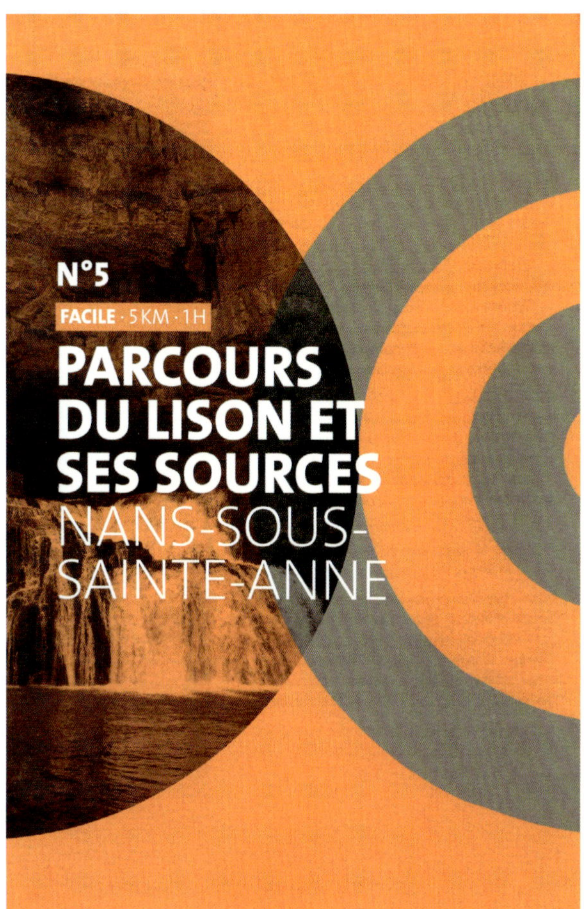

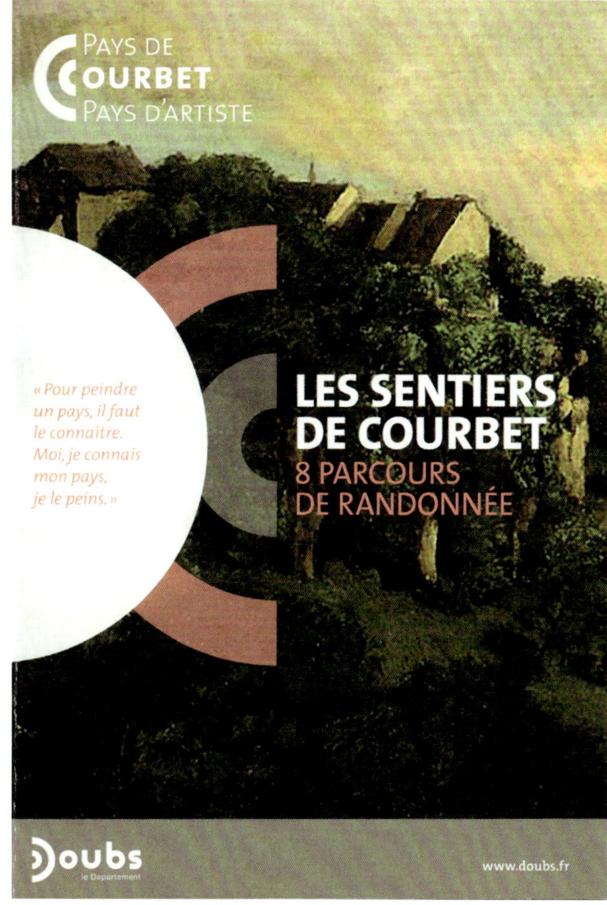

FIGS. 3.5, 3.6 Trail guides produced by the Department Doubs in 2012, including the brochure "Parcours du Lison et ses sources: Nans-sous-Sainte-Anne" (left), number five in a series of eight guides compiled in the book *Les Sentiers du Courbet: 8 parcours de randonnée* (right) written by Pascal Reilé.

cultural geography developed by scholars such as Denis Cosgrove and Stephen Daniels, we could say that Courbet's "symbolic landscapes" engendered the "material landscapes" modern tourists have come to admire. In turn, the latter sites' resemblance to Courbet's paintings have given them the status of "associative cultural landscapes." Present-day visitors to the Franche-Comté are invited to walk Courbet's paths (**FIGS. 3.5, 3.6**) in order to admire the "unspoiled" landscapes Courbet painted but, ironically, never saw as they appear today.

1. Recently restored, this atelier, designed by Courbet's friend Léon Isabey (1821–1895), is now open to the public.

2. Courbet's initial painting of the source of the Lison is mentioned in a letter by the artist to his parents, sent from Salins on November 27, 1864. See Petra ten-Doesschate Chu, *Correspondance de Courbet* (Paris: Flammarion, 1996), 222. Probably painted in October or early November 1864, its genesis is described by the artist's friend Max Claudet in the latter's *Souvenirs* (see note 12). This painting (see fig. 1.2), currently on loan to the Minnesota Marine Art Museum in Winona, is reproduced in Robert Fernier, *La Vie et l'oeuvre de Gustave Courbet: Catalogue raisonné* (Lausanne: Bibliothèque des arts; Fondation Wildenstein, 1977–78), 1:222, cat. no. 402. (Hereafter, paintings by Courbet will be indicated by "Fernier" followed by their number in the catalogue raisonné.) In the letter to his parents, Courbet also mentions that he made a reduced copy of *The Source of the Lison* for a M. Meyer (Fernier 403); it is now in an Italian private collection. Several other versions of the painting, not mentioned in Courbet's letters or other contemporary documents, exist, including the one owned by the University of Pennsylvania that is at the center of this exhibition (see fig. 1.1). Another was sold at Sotheby's, London, on December 16, 2015, lot 30 (Fernier, no number [unidentified paintings], 2:324); reproduced https://www.sothebys.com/en/auctions/ecatalogue/2014/19th-century-european-paintings-l15102/lot.30.html. Art historians disagree about the authenticity and the exact subject of *The Source of the Lison* in the Alte Nationalgalerie in Berlin (see fig. 1.3); reproduced https://commons.wikimedia.org/wiki/File:Berlin,_Alte_Nationalgalerie,_Gustave_Courbet,_die_Quelle_des_Lison.JPG. The same is true for a painting titled *Source du Lison près de Nans* (*Source of the Lison near Nans*), auctioned at Sotheby's, New York, on May 7, 2015, lot 71; reproduced https://www.sothebys.com/en/auctions/ecatalogue/2015/19th-century-european-art-n09342/lot.71.html. A signed and dated (1880) painting of the source of the Lison by Courbet's student Marcel Ordinaire was sold in Besançon on April 24, 2021, by the auction house of Astrid Guillon; see https://www.macommune.info/une-nouvelle-commissaire-priseur-organise-sa-premiere-vente-a-besancon.

3. Versions of *The Source of the Loue* (*La Source de la Loue*) are found in the collections of the Kunsthalle, Hamburg; Kunsthaus, Zürich; and Metropolitan Museum of Art, New York, among others. At least two paintings of the Chauveroche are known, both in private collections. *Le Gour de Conche* is now in the Musée des Beaux-Arts, Besançon. Courbet sold the painting to the Salins industrialist Alfred Bouvet, along with the only known version of *Le Fort de Joux*, now in a private collection. *The Grotto of Sarrazine near Nans-sous-Sainte-Anne* (ca. 1864) is in the J. Paul Getty Museum, Los Angeles.

4. On the economy of the Doubs department in the mid-nineteenth century, see Jean Luc Mayaud, *Les Secondes républiques du Doubs* (Paris: Les Belles Lettres, 1986).

5. Mayaud, *Les Secondes républiques*, 135.

6. On the concept of emulation in nineteenth-century France, see Carol E. Harrison, *The Bourgeois Citizen in Nineteenth-Century France: Gender, Sociability, and the Uses of Emulation* (Oxford Scholarship Online, October 2011), DOI: 10.1093/acprof:oso/9780198207771.001.0001.

7. Petra ten-Doesschate Chu, "'It Took Millions of Years to Compose That Picture,'" in *Courbet Reconsidered*, ed. Sarah Faunce and Linda Nochlin, exh. cat. (New Haven, CT: Yale University Press, 1988), 57.

8. Jules Marcou, "Les Géologues et la géologie du Jura jusqu'en 1870," *Mémoires de la Société d'émulation du Jura*, 4th ser., vol. 4 (1888): 119–200, trans. by the author.

9. Alexandre Brongiart, *Tableau des terrains qui composent l'écorce du globe ou essai sur la structure de la partie connue de la terre* (Paris: Levrault, 1829), 21. Marcou's own contribution, among others, was that he discovered Jurassic formations in other areas of the world, particularly in North America. See, for example, Jules Marcou, *Lettres sur les roches du Jura et leur distribution géographique dans les deux hémisphères* (Paris: Klincksieck, 1857–60).

10. Georges Riat, *Gustave Courbet* (Paris: Floury, 1906), 217.

11. For more on Marcou, Courbet, and the painting of *La Roche Pourrie*, see Petra ten-Doesschate Chu, "Courbet's La Roche Pourrie, Souvenir and Memento Mori," in *Gustave Courbet: L'École de la nature | The School of Nature*, ed. Carine Joly and Valérie Pugin, exh. cat. (Sivana: Cinisello Balsamo, 2021), 38–43.

12. Max Claudet, *Souvenirs: Gustave Courbet* (Paris: Dubuisson, 1878), 8–11.

13. Claudet, *Souvenirs*, 10, trans. by the author.

14. Paul Galvez, *Courbet's Landscapes: The Origins of Modern Painting* (New Haven, CT: Yale University Press, 2022), 146, has argued rightly that a careful study of Courbet's paintings reveals there was more to them than the "troweled masonry" of the palette knife. Indeed, the paint application in his landscapes was quite sophisticated and clearly shows a mixture of knife and brush. It is possible that the artist "laid in" the painting with the knife and, later, in the studio, finessed it with the brush.

15. Nathalie Vidal, "Charles Beauquier a-t-il sauvé la Source du Lison? Naissance d'une rumeur," in *Les Mondes de Beauquier*, ed. Noel Barbe (Besançon: Editions du Sekoya, 2015), 12–13. See also Claude-Isabelle Brelot and Jean-Luc Mayaud, *La Taillanderie de Nans-sous-Sainte-Anne* (Paris: Garnier, 1982), 42–43.

16. The print was produced by the lithographic establishment Valluet Jeune, in Besançon.

17. Courbet, on a few occasions, did depict industrial structures exploiting natural sites, as in *The Source of the Loue* in the Metropolitan Museum of Art, New York, or the *Papermill in Ornans* (*Papeterie d'Ornans*) in the Musée Courbet in Ornans. Neither painting bears a date, and although some art historians date them to 1864, I would argue that both were painted in the second half of the 1860s.

18. Quoted in Marcel Prévost, Joseph Bédier, and Raymond Recouly, "Un Témoin de la bohème littéraire," *La Revue de France* 5, no. 2 (1926): 86, trans. by the author.

19. Isabelle Brunnarius, "Assèchement du Doubs: Une histoire connue d'avance," *Le blog de la Loue et des rivières comtoises*, August 28, 2018, https://france3 -regions.blog.francetvinfo.fr /vallee-de-la-loue/2018/08/28 /assechement-du-doubs-une -histoire-connue-davance.html.

20. Jean-Paul Jacob and Michel Mangin, *De la Mine à la forge en Franche-Comté: Des origines au XIXe siècle* (Paris: Les Belles lettres, 1990), 146–47. The village of Nans-sous-Sainte-Anne had boasted a large metal tool factory since the 1830s; it survives in the Musée de la Taillanderie.

21. Chu, *Correspondance de Courbet*, 233, letter 65.5.

22. Charles Beauquier, *Philosophie de la musique* (Paris: Baillière, 1865), 158.

23. Beauquier, *Philosophie de la musique*, 158, trans. by the author.

24. Martha McCarey, "Aux Origines de la 'Loi Beauquier' pour la protection des paysages: Le pittoresque, la région et l'utilité publique," in Barbe, *Les Mondes de Beauquier*, 26, trans. by the author.

25. See Vidal, "Charles Beauquier," 15–16.

I have known landscapists intimidated by
solitude. The impression here is striking.
You can spend the entire day without seeing
a passerby. . . . The blue sky is hidden under
leafy branches, and even at noon sunlight
barely strikes the uppermost reaches. . . .
For how many more centuries will the
stream follow its course to the abyss? . . .
Will future ages rediscover the marvelous
surprise of these mysterious and
untouched woods?

—GASTON COINDRE, *LE VIEUX SALINS*

OF SOURCES AND SALT

PAUL GALVEZ

n his 1904 guidebook *Le Vieux Salins* (*Old Salins*), the Bisontine artist Gaston Coindre recounts his isolation before a waterfall outside the town. A visit to the nearby source of the Lison River, painted by Gustave Courbet in 1864 (see fig. 1.2), would have no doubt been just as eerie. For in front of the gaping cavern, we do not merely feel alone. We feel insignificant, as if the landscape, oblivious to our human sense of time and scale, had been this way since prehistoric times, when there were no people, and would still be far into the future, when humankind will most likely be extinct. To capture what might be called the landscape's inhuman temporality (as opposed to its timelessness, a term that connotes sentiment or ideality, and therefore a human frame of reference), Courbet excluded from his painting the mills, manufactories, and historic sites in the vicinity (**FIG. 4.1**).[1] This apparent disavowal of industry and history is striking for an artist known for his images of people and contemporary life. In order to shed light on Courbet's curious editing of the motif, we need to look more closely at "new" Salins, the artist's base of operations when he painted the source of the Lison in late 1864.

A useful guide is the local weekly newspaper, *Le Salinois*. The edition of four to eight pages, usually fronted by official pronouncements and a feuilleton, addressed all sorts of local news, with ads in the back (who knew the real estate market in 1860s Jura was so vibrant?). The publisher, Étienne Billet (and

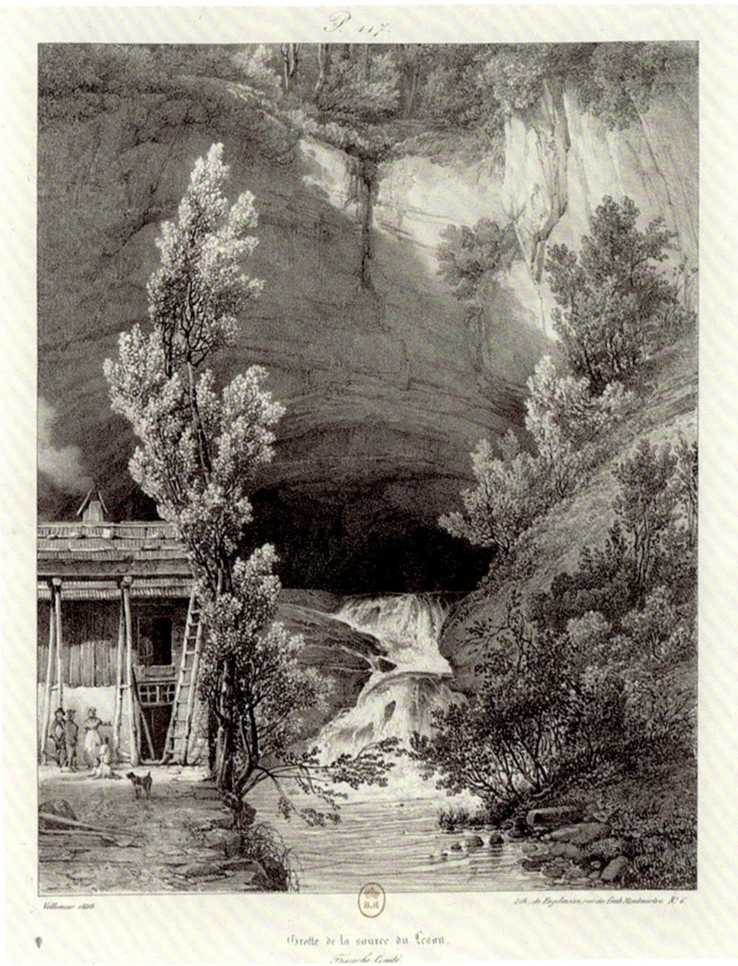

FIG. 4.1 Godefroy Engelmann, *Grotto of the Source of the Lison*, lithograph from Charles Nodier, Isidore-Justin-Séverin Taylor, and Achille-Alexandre-Alphonse de Cailloux de Cailleux, *Voyages pittoresques et romantiques dans l'ancienne France*, vol. 2, *Franche-Comté* (Paris: P. Didot l'aîné, 1825), pl. 117. Cleveland Art Museum: Twenty-fifth anniversary gift, Mr. and Mrs. Lewis B. Williams Collection, 1941.162.

later his son Victor), ran one of the town's three bookstores, and the printing house produced several texts by the Salinois writer Max Buchon, one of Courbet's close friends. We know that Buchon had actively promoted Courbet's painting in the local press during the Second Republic. When Victor Billet took over the running of the journal from his father in June 1864, Buchon became one of *Le Salinois*'s main contributors, a move that worried local officials due to the incitement he might cause.[2] Courbet's visit between September and December 1864 occurred just as *Le Salinois* was about to request authorization from the government to become a political newspaper. By staying in Salins, Courbet thus rekindled an alliance from his youth, when Buchon was also a journalist.

The earliest known reference to Courbet's paintings of the source of the Lison is, in fact, an announcement by Buchon in the newspaper's December 11, 1864, issue.[3] Two versions, one for a M. Meyer[4] and another (probably) for Buchon, were included in a list of current works that the author thought would make excellent material for a future exhibition in Salins (along the lines, perhaps, of a similar endeavor undertaken by Courbet in Saintes in 1863). Why was Buchon so eager to publicize Courbet's painting of the source at this particular moment? He was, of course, in the habit of promoting the artist, but usually in Parisian publications or his own literary journal.[5] To do so in the local newspaper implies further motivation.

First, some civic history. Salins in the nineteenth century was seemingly cursed. A conflagration in 1825 had decimated the town, then one of the most important in the region. More recently, a financial catastrophe during the year of Courbet's visit (perhaps precipitated by the collapse of one of the area's main industries, wine making, due to wildfires[6]) had led to a situation so dire that Salins's most prominent businessman (and Courbet collector) Alfred Bouvet stated on the front page of *Le Salinois* that he could no longer offer financial assistance to needy residents.[7]

Reflecting on this situation decades later, Coindre claimed Bouvet to have been one of Salins's saviors, alongside "the Virgin and M. Grimaldi."[8] The Mother of God's intercession on Salins's behalf being impossible to verify, let us turn to the role of Jean-Marie de Grimaldi in the town's affairs. Spanish by descent, Grimaldi was an ambitious businessman and imperial favorite. With the help of Queen Maria-Christina of Spain, he became administrator of the recently privatized Salines de l'Est in 1843 and worked for over a decade to monopolize salt production in the area, a feat finally achieved in 1862. Vertical integration was also key. In 1852, he obtained the rights to a rail line that would connect Salins to the main Dijon-Dôle-Besançon artery, making salt transport easier (and more profitable).

FIG. 4.2 *Le Salinois*, July 30, 1865, with list of
visitors who arrived July 21–28.

26ᵉ Année. — Nᵒ 31. (1865.) Dimanche 30 juillet.

LE SALINOIS

JOURNAL DE L'ARRONDISSEMENT DE POLIGNY,

Littéraire, Agricole, Commercial, PUBLIANT les Actes officiels et administratifs, les Nouvelles locales
les Annonces judiciaires et Avis divers.

Le SALINOIS paraît le **Dimanche**. — Prix de l'Abonnement, payable d'avance : Pour le Jura, un an, 7 fr.; — pour les autres départements, un an, 8 fr. — L'abonnement continue jusqu'à réception d'un avis contraire.
Prix des annonces : 15 centimes la ligne.

On reçoit les abonnements et annonces, à Salins, chez M. Bullet, imprimeur-libraire; à Paris, chez MM. Havas, Laffite, Bullier et Cie., rue J.-J. Rousseau, 5, et place de la Bourse; à Paris, chez M. Norbert-Estibal, place de la Bourse. *Affranchir.*
Les abonnements datent des 1ᵉʳ et 16 de chaque mois.

Le Salinois étant imprimé le samedi, on est prié de faire parvenir les annonces pour le vendredi matin.

BAINS DE SALINS. -- SAISON DE 1865.

6ᵉ liste des Etrangers arrivés aux eaux de Salins-les-Bains, du 21 au 28 juillet 1865.

NOMBRE.	NOMS.	PROFESSION.	DOMICILE.	INDICATION DU LOGEMENT.
report 421				
1	Mme Beaux,		Ornans.	M. Meyer.
2	M. et Mme Cassabois,		Paris.	maison Méraux.
1	Mme de Joux,		Savigny.	Etablissement des bains.
1	Mlle de Montilli,		id.	id.
1	Mlle Cluesmann,		Paris.	maison Cornu.
2	M. et Mme Ducommun,		Mulhouse.	maison Bousson.
1	M. Debias,		Pontroyal.	hôtel des Messageries.
1	Mlle Maubert,		Arbois.	maison Peschoud.
1	M. Breunne fils,		Dole.	Etablissement des bains.
1	Sœur Suzanne,		Poligny.	maison David.
1	Sœur Candide,		id.	id.
1	Mlle Ricaud-Mutin,		Dijon.	hôtel des Messageries.
1	Mme Goguely,		Baume-les-Dames	id
1	M. Chaudonnet,		Grancey-le-Chât.	Mme Lahute.
2	Mme et Mlle Pignolet,		Beaune.	hôtel du Commerce.
6	Mmes et Mlles Veipert,		Paris.	maison Pillot.
4	M. et Mmes Barry et une bonne,			Etablissement des bains.
1	Mme Huot,		Arbois.	Arbois.
1	Mme Bellenand,		Chalons-s-Saône.	hôtel des Messageries.
1	Mme Harnoux,		id.	id.
1	M. Bousson,		Paris.	maison Bousson.
2	M. et Mme de Renneville,		id.	M. Duperron.
1	M. Boigeat,		Rougemont.	hôtel des Messageries.
1	M. Kremer,		Paris.	hôtel du Sauvage.
3	M. et Mme de Chalonge et une bonne,		Pernand.	maison Billey.
2	M. et Mlle Nicolas,		Dole.	maison Maubert.
1	M. Bellon,		Paris.	hôtel des Messageries.
1	M. et Mme Dombey,		Pont-de-Veyle.	Etablissement des bains.
2	M. et Mme Lauer,		Paris.	id.
11	Baigneurs de Salins ou des environs,			
477	Ensemble,			

ARRÊTE :

Le nombre des conseillers à élire les 29 et 30 juillet est porté à CINQ.
Hôtel-de-Ville de Salins, le 28 juillet 1865.
Le Maire,
J. DE GRIMALDI.

Nous lisons dans le *Journal du Jura* :
Conseillers municipaux, élus le 23 juillet à Salins.

MM. Tournier, Louis	. . . .	1130
Toubin, Jules.	. . . .	1121
Varéchon, Remy.	. . . .	1116
Barbet, Clément .	. . .	1107
Satet, Louis	. . . .	1084
Besson, Joseph	. . . .	1077
Didier, Sébastien.	. . .	1061
Bouvet, Alfred	. . . .	1026
De Grimaldi .	. . .	895
Guignet, Henry	. . . .	757
Bonnet, Frédéric.	. . .	670
Courbet	. . . . .	649
De Lapomarède	. . . .	629
Toubin, Claude.	. . . .	618
Rodet, Henry.	. . . .	602
Thurel-Chamecin	. . .	598
Champon, Jules	. . .	598
Paul Dulman.	. . .	584
Pétament	. . . . .	581

Nous apprenons que le candidat élu, démissionnaire, serait M. Varéchon, adjoint au maire.

Nos lecteurs apprendront avec le plus grand plaisir que notre cher sculpteur jurassien Perraud, dont le talent est si pur et si élevé, vient d'être présenté en *première ligne* par la section de sculpture, pour la place devenue vacante à l'académie des Beaux-Arts par le décès de M. Duret.

Collége de Salins.

BULLETIN HEBDOMADAIRE.

Ont obtenu le 1ᵉʳ rang pour le travail :
(*Cours classiques.*)

Philo.rhétor. et 2ᵉ, — Edgar Boulangier.
3ᵉ, — Réné Toubin.

Grimaldi's activities also transformed Salins's urban fabric.
He converted part of the saltworks from which the town derives
its name into a bathing resort. The baths of the newly christened
Salins-les-bains officially opened on June 6, 1858, with much
pomp and circumstance (although the resort had already opened
to the public in 1854).[9] The baths dominated the summer
seasons, and the newspaper printed a weekly list of visitors,
noting where they lodged and their city of origin (**FIG. 4.2**).

Buchon had mixed feelings about Grimaldi's attempt to
make the Second Empire vogue for hydrotherapy part of Salins's
identity. In guidebooks directly aimed at the new visitors,
Buchon praised Grimaldi for funding things like the baths and
new walking paths near the source of the Lison.[10] But he also

complained in *Le Salinois* about the resort's noisy entertainment, made tongue-in-cheek remarks about the clientele, and eventually would distance himself from the project altogether.[11]

Buchon made his wariness about the investor-politician explicit in January 1865, when Grimaldi was nominated to replace the recently deceased mayor, Vicomte de Reculot. In a guarded endorsement, Buchon called Grimaldi both a "man of the government" and a "man of the town," underscoring the nominee's perceived mixed allegiances.[12] The writer begrudgingly gave the nominee his approval on the condition of more government transparency, ideally via published minutes of city council meetings in *Le Salinois*.

Buchon was in a difficult situation. He did not want to give the government's man unconditional support. But what else could save Salins if not Grimaldi's money? Luckily, the skeptical Buchon had a plan B: to rally support not from outside investors but from the local populace itself. If the baths were a less-than-ideal solution at a time of crisis, perhaps civic consciousness and social reforms could make up for loss of income and a shrinking population. Buchon had already tried to reinvigorate and institutionalize regional arts and letters through public subscriptions for civic monuments and the establishment of a journal devoted to popular literature.[13]

In September 1864—that is, just as Courbet was arriving for his three-month stay in Salins—the writer singled out other savants who, in his view, were just as important to Salins as Grimaldi.[14] These men—the sculptor Max Claudet, the geologist Jules Marcou, the college professor Charles Toubin, and Buchon himself—were all members of what the critic Jules Castagnary would later dub the town's "*colonie réaliste*" and were Courbet's constant companions during his visit.[15] As Courbet painted, Buchon and company organized. Reports on their activities in *Le Salinois* stand out among the usual town chatter. Their various proposals included improved municipal cemetery access, compulsory musical education, a new municipal library, and a

review of the bread tax.[16] They also kept the public abreast of
the "colony's" recent publications in science, literature,
and archeology.[17] In what ways, if any, could landscape painting
contribute to a new local consciousness?

Courbet's Source paintings seemingly avoid the town's
"politics of water." There was no direct or essential relationship
between source and saltworks; the Lison did not supply the
baths, and the grotto was just one of many sites for tourists to
visit. I have argued elsewhere that certain Source paintings were
Courbet's attempts at visualizing a subject dear to the "realist
colony": the search for origins.[18] Whether it be the ancient
etymology of a word or the epochal stratification of a rock,
Courbet and his friends believed that the painstaking
examination of seemingly simple objects could reveal the hidden
processes of their formation. This required enormous effort on
the part of the investigator. But the rewards were great. Previously
unknown and repressed stages of history could be resurrected.
The microstudy could reveal the mechanism of larger historical
forces.[19] The viewer of a Courbet landscape could be considered
a visual archeologist examining the world in close detail in order
to unearth its various layers. As many have noted, this is partly
an effect of Courbet's unique palette-knife technique, in which
skin-like touches are overlaid to generate the illusion of great
mass. However, unlike the actual painted surface, which almost
never exceeds more than three layers of paint marks, the depicted
landscape appears constituted by a seemingly infinite number of
forms emerging from darkness. We are led to believe that
Courbet painted much more thickly than he actually did because
his landscapes produce the *illusion* of unfathomable depth.
This is possible because the image does not collapse into pure
paint at close range. Extraordinarily, paint strokes still read as
rock, water, and moss, even when viewed up close. Thus, the
illusion remains convincing for far longer than most painting at
the time was capable of at comparable distance. And it is this
experience of perceptual duration, more than the actual thickness
of paint, that accounts for the strange feeling of encountering a

mysterious world continuously emanating from the depths of the picture, as if peering back into deep time.

This prolonged, focused, and multilayered engagement with the world was a direct response to the anomie of modern life, including the superficial experience and false promise of satisfaction offered by tourism. *The Source of the Lison* renounced society because it was trying to imagine a different way of relating to the world that was not one of the domination of nature and struggle for control. That subsequent history has taught us the hopelessness of that dream does not diminish the singularity of Courbet's attempt to realize it. His Source paintings could be considered part of a last-ditch effort at revitalizing—but also transforming—romantic nature, a task that had become increasingly desperate by the 1860s. The work's physical intensity demonstrates the extremes to which one had to go in order to produce from within existing landscape traditions the illusion of a non-alienated, substantive relationship to one's surroundings. In 1864, Courbet's circle still maintained the belief that such a condition was possible, and that it might survive side-by-side or even flourish in the face of modern leisure—that is, they believed that the Buchons and the bathers of the world could coexist, especially by paying close attention to language and landscape.[20]

Thus, forming an accurate picture of a particular set of current social relations, however desirable, was not the primary motor driving the Buchon circle's critical and artistic activities (although it certainly empowered their political ones). What linked the various intellectual endeavors advertised in *Le Salinois*, including Courbet's painting, was a more general attitude to analyzing the past: one shared by other historicizing discourses of the nineteenth century (historical materialism included), one that would treat the local as a dynamic engine of change rather than as a quaint set of static, outmoded practices.

To gauge the difference between Courbet and other artistic attempts at reconnection with nature, let us look at the Barbizon School painter Théodore Rousseau and his image of the source of the Lison. Rousseau's father, Pierre-Catherine Rousseau,

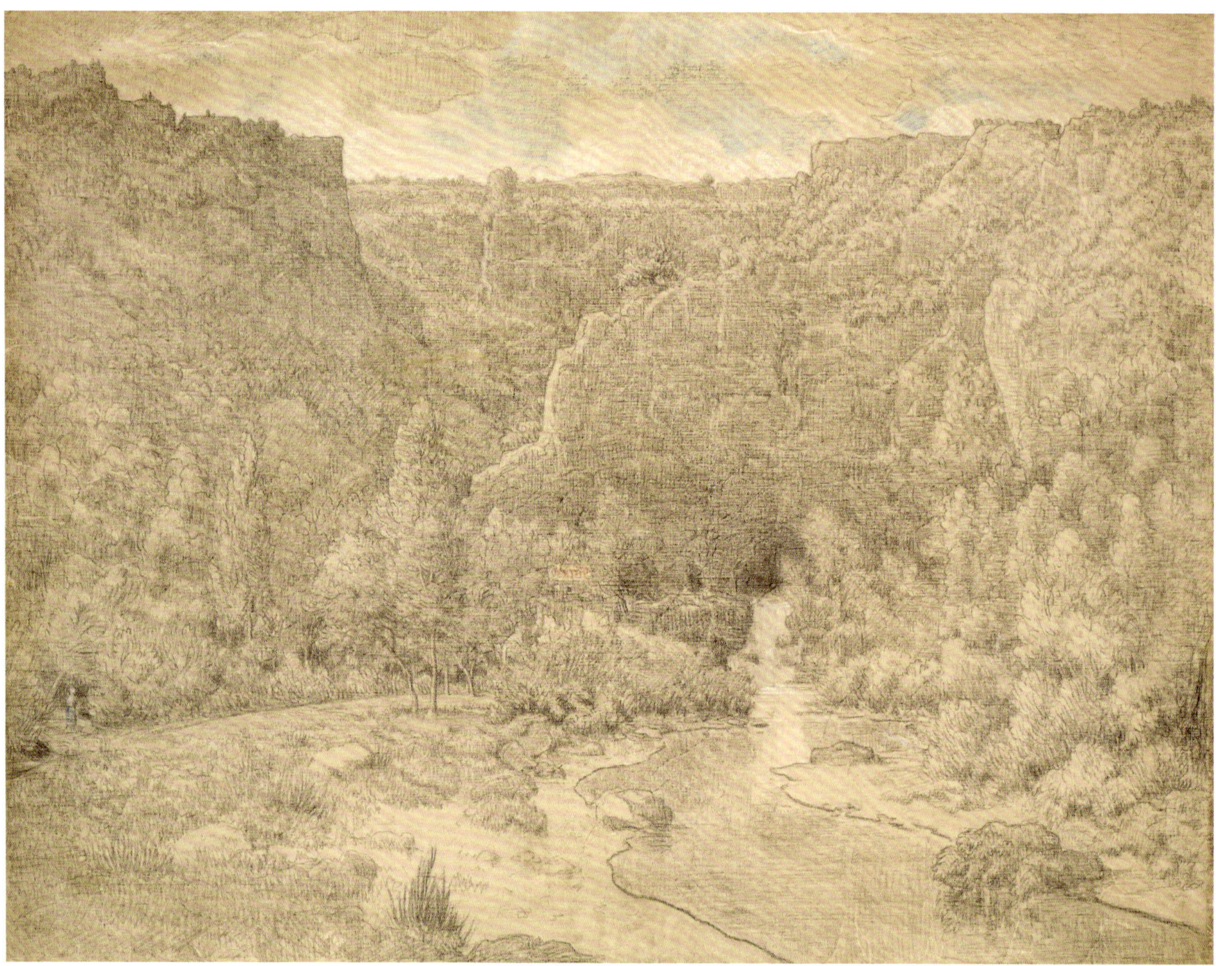

FIG. 4.3 Théodore Rousseau, *The Source of the River Lison (Doubs)*, ca. 1863, charcoal on canvas, with heightening, 35 ¼ × 45 ¹¹⁄₁₆ in. (89.5 × 116 cm). Musée du Louvre, MNR 202.

was from Salins (a fact that is mentioned at least once in *Le Salinois*).[21] Rousseau visited the region several times, as numerous drawings of the surrounding countryside attest. One bout of sketching in the area (most likely during one of the trips of the early 1860s) led to the making of a full-scale ébauche of the source of the Lison (**FIG. 4.3**). Rousseau's image of the site is typical of the artist in panoramic mode. From a high vantage point above the Lison River unfurls a natural expanse. Usually, Rousseau's sketches either isolate a small landscape area for focused examination or, on the contrary, capture an overall atmospheric mood, glossing over individual details. His highly developed ébauche *The Source of the River Lison (Doubs)* combines the two modes. It is at once a microscopic study of tiny details and a macroscopic view of the world at large. Though Rousseau locates the viewpoint at considerable distance from the water-spouting cavern for which the drawing is named, there is hardly any part of the composition upon which the artist has not lavished the most exacting care, as if we were observing each landscape element from up close. One can make out single blades of grass in the foreground, tree trunks and branches in the midground, and even leafy outgrowths on the distant cliffs. Moreover, lest the singular detail distract us too much from the whole, Rousseau has delineated the landscape's primary contours, as if revealing a hidden template: dark black lines define the banks of a river as it courses out of the picture; the righthand cliff is decisively traced where it hits sky and ground, respectively. Rousseau's working process is twofold: first, draw with charcoal and pastel; then, complete with oil pigments. *Source of the Lison* testifies to a general principle of his work: painting comes after drawing; that is, the material application of paint follows the creation of a delineated, drawn prototype that precedes it both formally and conceptually.

The difference from Courbet's *The Source of the Lison* (*La Source du Lison*) of 1864 (see fig. 1.2) is so dramatic that one almost doesn't recognize that they depict the same site. It is not as if Courbet was unaware of or had never been interested by the panoramic view. A drawing (**FIG. 4.4**) from one of his early sketchbooks testifies to a youthful fascination with just the kind of delineation pursued by Rousseau (notice the doubly-thick left edge of the rock formation housing the source, strikingly similar in its prominence to the same feature in the Rousseau). In the Rousseau, the grotto is an obscure, almost negligible black patch; in the Courbet, it is an outsized hole at the center of the visual field. Even more fundamental is the difference in conceptual approach. Whereas Rousseau overlays a preconceived template with brushed paint, Courbet generates his landscape without drawing as an intermediary. From an as-yet-unformed dark ground, visibly discrete palette-knife and brush deposits slowly

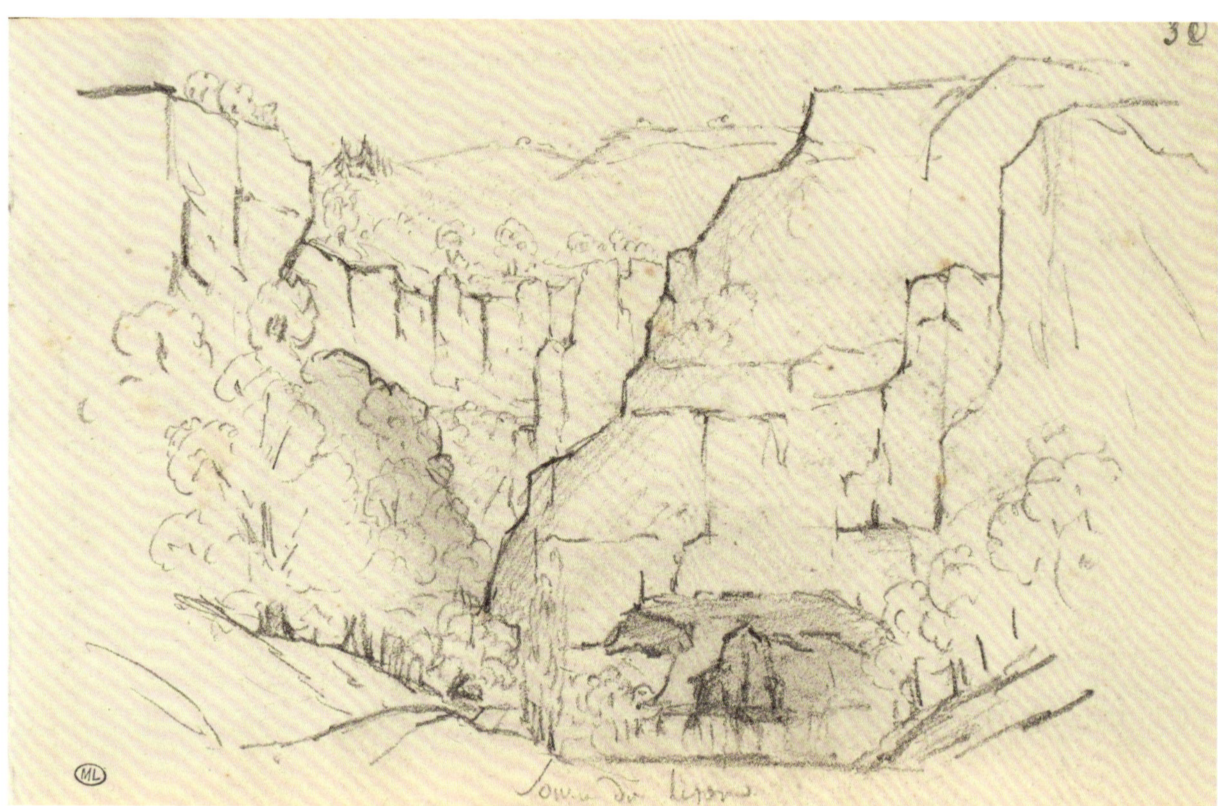

arise across the canvas, as if being illuminated by the morning sun at dawn, to paraphrase Max Claudet's firsthand account of Courbet painting the source of the Lison.[22]

Beyond formal considerations, it would be intriguing in a future study to compare what has been called Rousseau's "ecological" approach to landscape with Courbet's own. Scholars have detected a preservationist streak emanating from the milieus of both artists.[23] Rousseau fought for the protection of the forest of Fontainbleau. Charles Beauquier, a Franc-comtois music critic and follower of Courbet, helped establish one of France's first environmental protection laws (enacted to protect the source of the Loue River, an earlier motif that had prepared Courbet for painting the source of the Lison).[24] Already in Courbet's time, the politics of conservation underwent a familiar split, as we can see in the contrasting fates of Beauquier and Coindre, the author of *Le Vieux Salins*, whose landscape description opened this essay. Beauquier's interest in local culture led to his election as a Republican deputy battling to protect the

FIG. 4.4 Gustave Courbet, *Mountain Landscape: The Source of the Lison*, from *Album Gustave Courbet* no. 2, graphite on paper, 5 ½ × 8 9⁄16 in. (14 × 21.7 cm). Musée d'Orsay, RF 29234-35, folio 30.

landscape from overdevelopment, not unlike Rousseau's own motives (despite the differences in artistic execution between the latter's and Courbet's Sources). Coindre's primary legacy was to be the illustrator of the books of Édouard Drumont, the antisemitic founder of the journal *Libre parole* (*Free Speech*). On the one hand (the left one), nature was conceived as an open and collective resource, subject to competing social forces and changing needs and, in Courbet's case, as a model for historical analysis; and on the other hand, the right naturalized "nature," turning it into a nostalgic fantasy of a world that had never been, and the new "free speech" adopted for its own purposes the language of the old town.

This essay expands upon arguments put forth in my book *Courbet's Landscapes: The Origins of Modern Painting* (2022). I thank Lynn Marsden-Atlass and André Dombrowski for the opportunity to present material not included in that earlier study.

Epigraph: Gaston Coindre, *Le Vieux Salins: Promenades et causeries* (Besançon: Jacquin, 1904), 363.

1. Compare with the descriptions of the source in Charles Nodier, Justin Taylor, and Alphonse de Cailleux, *Voyages pittoresques et romantiques dans l'ancienne France*, vol. 2, *Franche-Comté* (Paris: J. Didot l'aîné, 1825), 163–65.

2. Letter from prefect Beauregard to the Minister of the Interior, March 30, 1865, National Archives of France, AN F18 466, as cited in Marcel Vogne, *La Presse périodique en Franche-Comté: Des Origines à 1870* (Vanves: M. Vogne, 1977), 4:294. On Buchon's earlier journalism, see T. J. Clark, *Image of the People: Gustave Courbet and the 1848 Revolution*, 3rd edition (Berkeley: University of California Press, 1999), 109–13.

3. Max Buchon, "Lettre salinoise," *Le Salinois*, December 11, 1864.

4. *Le Salinois*, September 18, 1864, reported that a certain Charles Meyer was named police commissioner on September 6, 1864. Was this the Meyer mentioned by Buchon?

5. A version of Buchon's announcement was published in "Lettre salinoise," *Union des arts*, December 17, 1864. Buchon's journal was *Revue littéraire de la Franche-Comté*.

6. *Le Salinois*, August 21, 1864.

7. *Le Salinois*, August 14, 1864.

8. Coindre, *Le Vieux Salins*, 147.

9. Typical of the over-the-top official reporting on the baths was an open letter by the president of the Conseil général and deputy Edouard Dalloz, which was published in *Le Moniteur*, October 8 and 15, 1864, and in "Salins-les-bains," *Le Salinois*, October 9 and 16, 1864, describing a hasty visit, led by Grimaldi, to the baths in September. On that visit, see *Le Salinois*, September 4, 1864.

10. Max Buchon, *Salins-les-Bains: Ses eaux minérales et ses environs* (Lons-le-Saunier: de Gauthier frères, 1862; new ed. Salins: Billet, 1866), 19, 50.

11. On the increasing enmity between Buchon and Grimaldi, see Max Buchon, *Lettres Salinoises* (Salins: Billet, 1866).

12. Buchon, "Lettre salinoise," *Le Salinois*, January 22, 1865.

13. *Le Salinois*, July 17 and 31, October 22, and December 16, 1864; *Revue littéraire de la Franche-Comté*, first issue announced in *Le Salinois*, September 20, 1863.

14. *Le Salinois*, September 25, 1864.

15. Courbet Papers, Bibliothèque nationale de France, BnF Yb3-1739, box 4.

16. *Le Salinois*, January 29–March 5, April 23–May 14, 1865.

17. Petra ten-Doesschate Chu, "It Took Millions of Years to Compose That Picture," in *Courbet Reconsidered*, ed. Sarah Faunce and Linda Nochlin, exh. cat. (New Haven, CT: Yale University Press, 1988), 55–66.

18. Paul Galvez, *Courbet's Landscapes: The Origins of Modern Painting* (New Haven, CT: Yale University Press, 2022).

19. This would echo the distinction Toubin made between "positivist" knowledge (essentially, fact gathering) and "positive" knowledge (i.e., critical interpretation) in a speech delivered at the college of Salins, "Discours prononcé par M. Charles Toubin à la distribution des prix au collège," *Le Salinois*, August 13, 1865.

20. Bathers were encouraged to learn about local patois by purchasing

Buchon's *Nöels et chansons de la Franche-Comté* (Salins: Billet, 1863), see *Le Salinois*, July 26, 1863, and "Bibliographie," *Le Salinois*, November 15, 1863; and also to peruse the geological collection in the baths' library donated by Claude-Marie Germain, Marcou's mentor, see *Le Salinois*, "Salins-les-bains," October 16, 1864.

21. "Discours prononcé par M. Charles Toubin."

22. Max Claudet, *Souvenirs: Gustave Courbet* (Paris: Dubuisson, 1878), 8–11.

23. Greg M. Thomas, *Art and Ecology in Nineteenth-Century France: The Landscapes of Théodore Rousseau* (Princeton, NJ: Princeton University Press, 2000); and Stephen Eisenman and Charles F. Stuckey, *From Corot to Monet: The Ecology of Impressionism* (Milan: Skira, 2010).

24. Noël Barbe, ed., *Les Mondes de Beauquier* (Besançon: Sékoya), 2014.

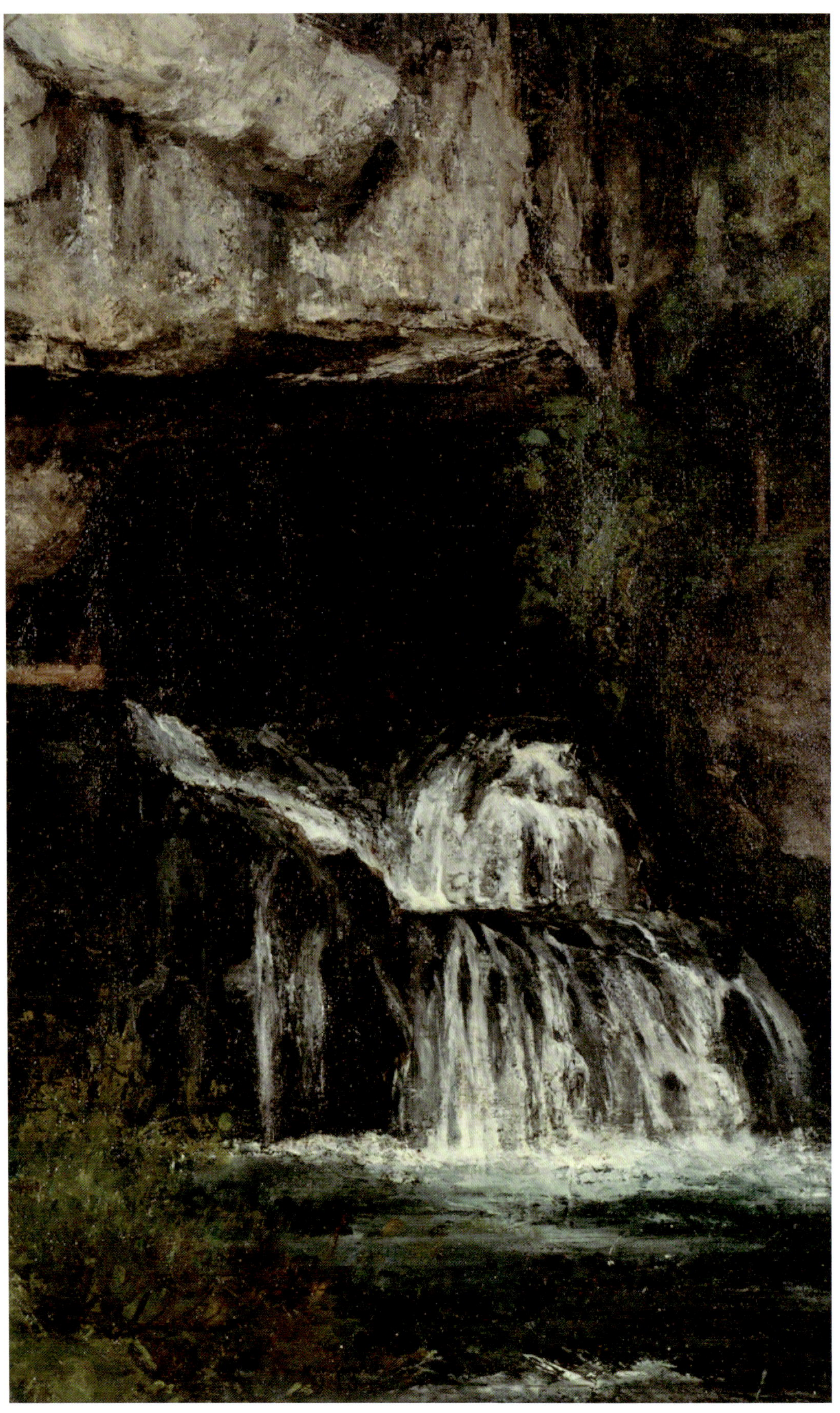

COURBET PAINTING IN NATURE

MARY MORTON

French artists have been sketching in nature at least since the seventeenth century, but the practice of bringing oil paints outdoors to capture light effects and textures beyond the capacity of graphite became common only in the years around 1800. Completing their artistic education in Rome, artists from across Europe fanned out in the countryside in and around the ancient city recording their visual impressions quickly, in oil, on pieces of paper and board. Thousands of miles from their native academies, in the sunny central Italian climate, they improvised using the tools at hand to respond to the tonal planes and colored light surrounding them. The resulting oil sketches were generally discarded, but occasionally the artists retained them as notes to inform future studio production. Not until the 1860s, in the hands of Gustave Courbet, was oil painting outdoors identified as a practice worthy of the highest form of French artistic production, brought from the margins to the center of advanced painting (**FIG. 5.1**). This essay outlines the art-world changes—institutional, critical, economic—that enabled this shift, and the degree to which this art historical event depended not only on particular historical conditions but also on the singular, catalytic persona of Courbet himself.

Although the preeminent French landscape painter of the later eighteenth century, Claude-Joseph Vernet, advocated oil sketching outdoors, the neoclassical painter and theorist Pierre Henri de Valenciennes was the major figure in establishing the

FIG 5.1 Detail, fig. 1.1

tradition. In a treatise published in 1799, he elevated the genre
of landscape painting to a refined humanist pursuit by subjecting
it to the academic rules of rhetoric and perspective.[1] In a relatively
slim section of his voluminous tome, he also mandated oil
sketching outdoors, insisting on the necessity of attending to
all aspects of the landscape, from rocks to trees to waterfalls.
Particularly for sketches that include the sky, according to
Valenciennes, rapid capture was key in order to keep up with
changing light conditions: artists should spend no more than
two hours in a single sitting.

Valenciennes's volume was perhaps *the* central textbook for
artists learning landscape painting throughout the nineteenth
century, and it was key to formalizing the role of outdoor
sketching in the artistic curriculum. As an actual activity, however,
painting outdoors was extra-academic, practiced far from the
centralized, official authority of art professors, free of the
routinized, methodical practice of the studio, the dictates of
the reproductive print, the static plaster, the old-master model.
Setting up impromptu easels in the clear light and warm climate
of Italy, young artists from northern Europe set about transcribing
the sights, inventing techniques to economize their time and
accommodate the limited range of tools they carried with them:
a few brushes, a palette knife perhaps, rags, maybe the cork from a
wine bottle. Immersed in nature, they pushed the physical
properties of oil paint to maximum effect, layering and smearing
the still-wet paint with their fingers and brush, dabbing it with
a sponge for texture or to denote foliage, and engaging the
support, naked or toned, to fill out their compositions. Often
inspiring one another as they shared their results at the end
of the day, they could develop a fresh personal vision and
autographic technique.

Nearly four decades before Courbet painted the University
of Pennsylvania's *Source of the Lison* (*Source du Lison*; see fig. 1.1),
André Giroux hiked out of the hill town of Papigno north of
Rome into an overgrown, rocky creek bed to paint *Forest Interior
with Waterfall, Papigno* (*Intérieur de la forêt avec une chute d'eau,*

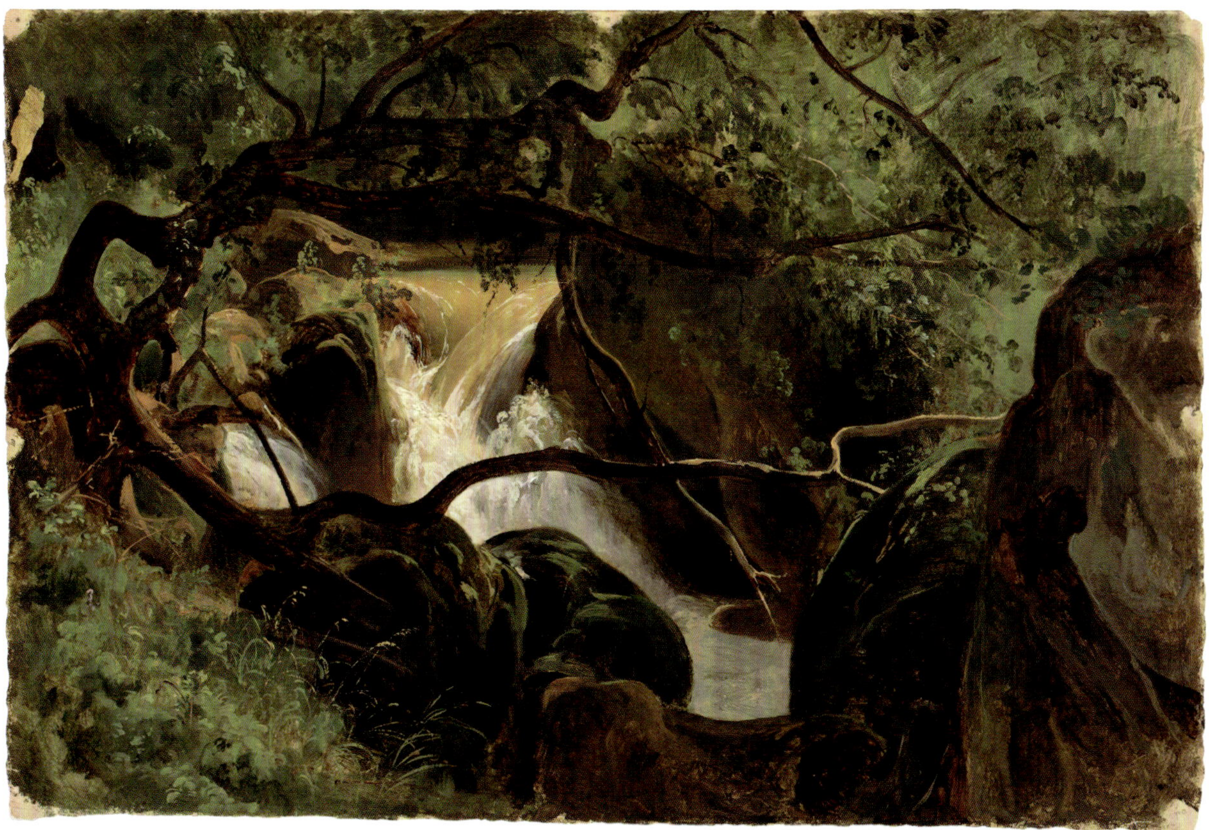

Papigno; **FIG. 5.2**). One imagines the artist energized by the physicality of the effort as well as by the visual thrill of rushing water and light filtering through dense green foliage, dashing off the scene in less than an hour. The image is immersive, boulders looming in the foreground, bare branches stretching across the painting toward the light. Giroux applied thin washes, long drags of opaque paint, delicate strokes with a pointed brush and stippled marks to convey the textures of rock, limb, leaf, grass, and stream. Around the same time, Christian Ernst Bernhard Morgenstern traveled into the Alps to capture *Waterfall on the River Traun, Upper Austria* (**FIG. 5.3**). On a small sheet of paper, he captured his experience of the explosive chute of water, his paint marks mimicking the spraying churn and conjuring the distinctive gray-green color of the fall's underside. Although they maintained a sense of composition, these artists clearly opened up to their motifs, improvising and inventing their own painterly vocabulary. Eschewing concerns extraneous to the moment—

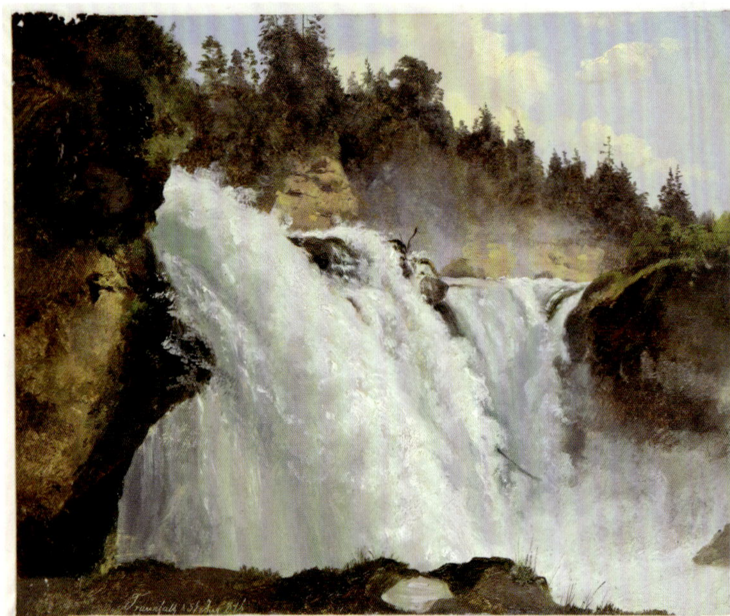

FIG. 5.3 Christian Ernst Bernhard Morgenstern, *Waterfall on the River Traun, Upper Austria*, 1826, oil on canvas, 11 × 14 ⅜ in. (28 × 36.4 cm). Fondation Custodia, Collection Frits Lugt, Paris, 2019-S.16.

such as studio conventions, narratives, and legible meaning itself—the resulting imagery is fresh and lively. This singular creative process, combining painterly innovation and a personal response to natural phenomena, afforded a level of individual freedom that would inevitably be constricted by the formal institutions to which these artists would return. Official studio practice, where the product was carefully controlled as artists submitted to the dictates of state, church, and private patrons, relegated such plein-air oil sketches as mere preparatory works. Of little to no value within the oeuvre of professional artists, they occasionally survived in their estates, sometimes traded or sold among fellow artists or to a handful of interested collectors. But the vast majority of these small pictures have been lost, and for over a century, the tradition of oil painting in nature itself was largely left out of art historical narratives.[2]

Landscape painting was the least prestigious genre in a hierarchy that, since the seventeenth century, had revered "grand manner" painting centered around the human figure arranged on the canvas in narrative tableaux. Courbet had every intention of participating in the most ambitious mode of painting, and he established a reputation for large-scale figural work early in his career, from *After Dinner at Ornans* (*L'Après-dinée à Ornans*; 1849, Palais des Beaux-Arts de Lille) to *A Burial at Ornans* (*Un enterrement à Ornans*; 1849–50, Musée d'Orsay, Paris), *Young Ladies of the Village* (*Les Demoiselles de village*; 1851–52, Metropolitan Museum of Art, New York), and *Young Ladies on the Banks of the Seine (Summer)* (*Les Demoiselles des bords de la Seine [été]*; 1857, Petit Palais, Paris). Notoriously bucking the system with his realist subject matter and unconventional compositions, he alternately railed against and reveled in resistance from official governing bodies. By the early 1860s, however, he became increasingly frustrated with what he considered to be a lack of official affirmation, and having signaled the importance of landscape painting to his sense of self as an artist in his epic *The Painter's Studio* (*L'Atelier du peintre*; **FIG. 5.4**) the previous decade, he retreated to his native region of the Jura in southeast France. During an extended campaign in 1863–65, he created an extraordinary body of work inspired by painting on site, outdoors. Attaching a cart with his art supplies to a donkey named Gérôme

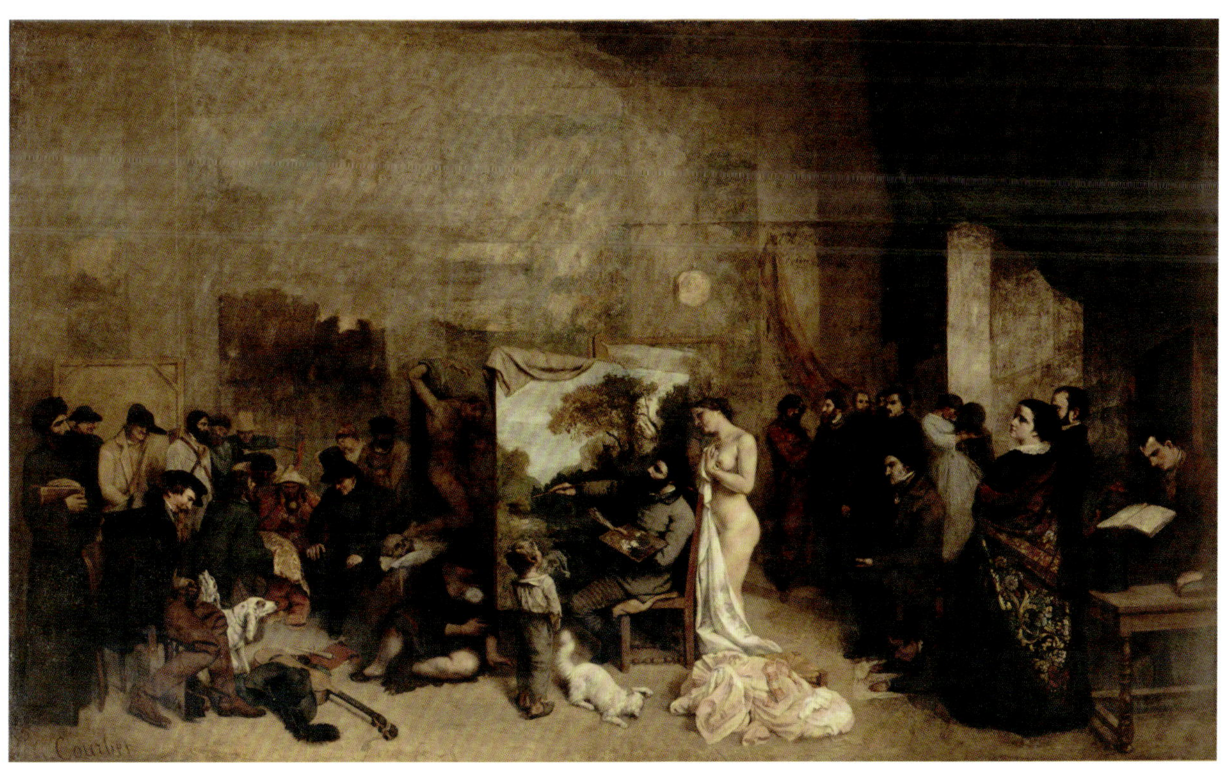

FIG. 5.4 Gustave Courbet, *The Painter's Studio*, 1854–55, oil on canvas, 142 ⅛ × 235 ⁷⁄₁₆ in. (361 × 598 cm). Musée d'Orsay, RF 2257.

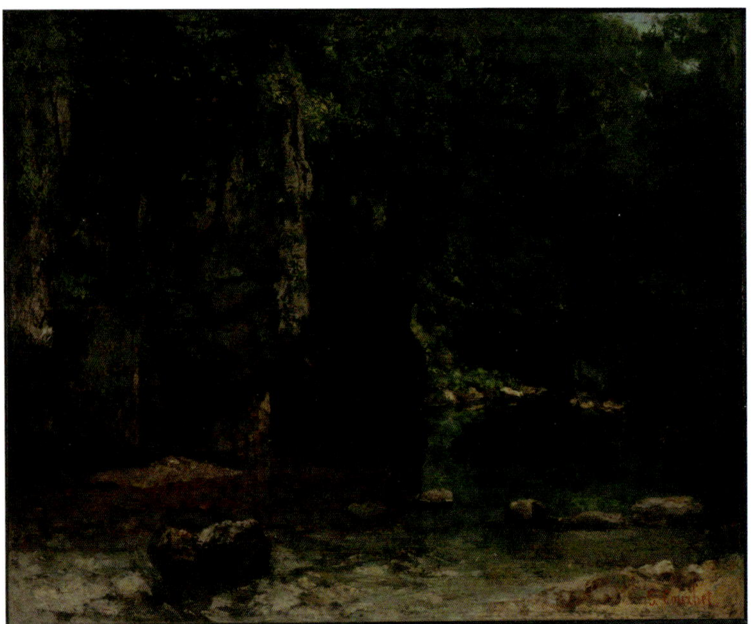

(after the most successful academic artist of the day, Jean-Léon Gérôme), he set out on foot to paint sylvan sites of the countryside around Ornans: the Puits-noir (**FIG. 5.5**), the rocks at Chauveroche, the source of the Loue River (see fig. 7.2) and the grotto of Sarrazine near Nans-sous-Sainte-Anne. In the fall of 1864, his close friend Max Claudet accompanied him on his hike to the source of the Lison where, he recounts, Courbet improvised with his palette knife, sponges and rags, and his fingers to complete, in two hours, a canvas one meter in size (see fig. 1.2).[3] Building up from a dark ground, Courbet alternated transparent glazes with thin skins of opaque paint to describe the craggy facets of the rock face, the clinging velvet moss, and the flowing cascade reflected in a pristine pool. Like Giroux and Morgenstern, he exploited the range of physical properties and possibilities of oil paint to create a powerfully sensual image of the scene's presence. As with his Puits-noir paintings and his other images of caves and rock faces, and above all in his extraordinary snowscapes, this version of the *Source of the Lison*, now in Minnesota, is unprecedented in palette, spatial composition and paint handling, informed equally by the artist's technical mastery, experimental energy, and intense response to the immanent natural motif.

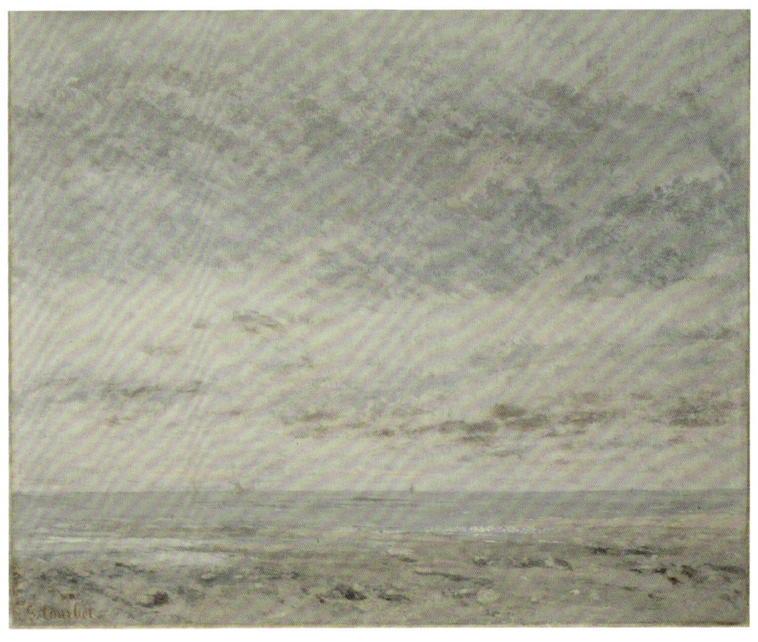

FIG. 5.6 Gustave Courbet, *Low Tide at Trouville*, ca. 1865, oil on canvas, 23 ½ × 28 ⅝ in. (84.5 × 96.5 cm), framed. Walker Art Gallery, Liverpool, purchased by the Walker Art Gallery with the assistance of Art Fund in 1961.

In the summer of 1865, Courbet visited the Channel coast and created his first series of minimalist marine pictures, calling them *paysages de mer* or "landscapes of the sea" (**FIG. 5.6**). Like his Jura landscapes, these paintings involved no preparatory work, no drawing or retouching, just focused sessions looking at the beach. Painting quickly became more urgent, given the mercurial coastal conditions; combined with the serial nature of the enterprise, this rapid execution emphasized the instinctual, phenomenological aspect of the exercise. For contemporaneous critics as well as later art historians, the Trouville paintings are distinguished by their personal, intuitive character, quintessentially "authentic" and "truthful" in their autographic essence.[4] This aesthetic of the sketch—the sense of spontaneity in loose brushwork and idiosyncratic compositions and subjects, and the element of experimentation and private self-realization— moved from a subordinating, preparatory role to the main performance, from ancillary notation to final products made for public exhibition.

This shift was encouraged by Naturalist critics of the 1860s who advocated for liberty, healthy vitality, regeneration, and sincerity in art and literature.[5] The values of the plein-air tradition, which emphasized empiricism and personal vision, were absorbed into a political campaign within contemporary art circles against the idealizing falsifications and pretentions of Salon painting and its association with old aristocratic and religious authorities.[6] Within a discourse denouncing the urban decadence, "spleen," and effeminacy of French art and society, the audacious individuality and vitality of a figure like Courbet—his physical and spiritual connection to the land as a hunter, fisherman, hiker, swimmer, painter—was picked up as an antidote to be valorized. Rescuing French painting from the death throes of history painting, with its obsolete ideas and delicate taste, Courbet proposed concrete, living images that privileged the personal eye, fugitive sensations, and nuanced, rich coloration.[7]

Having established an aggressive public persona, the "most arrogant man in France" found in landscape the perfect genre for self-referentiality. He cultivated an image of himself in the public press that corresponded directly to his landscapes: instinctual, sensual, confident, and free. And the land of the Franche-Comté itself, with its traditional spirit of political independence combined with immersive topographical motifs (canyons, forests, caves), provided an ideal source of nature images. "Never before has the work of a painter been a more faithful image of the character of the man," claimed Théodore Duret in 1867.[8]

By the end of the decade, the collective concerns of Courbet's socially and politically engaged figural works, the provocative commentaries on class, religion, gender, and power, had largely ceded center stage to autographic landscape paintings expressive of his "brand." Following the economic boom of the 1850s and the development in the 1860s of the distinct economic practice of art dealing, the market was primed for Courbet's saleable pictures, commodities that conveyed the individualist values of Second Empire industrial capitalism.[9] Courbet self-consciously redefined the role of the artist from a self-effacing public servant to an independent creative genius, eliding the academic tradition of reference and emulation in favor of fresh vision and unmediated perception. The ideals represented by the state system—civic and familial duty, piety, and public service—were supplanted by more atomized, transactional values encouraged by the market, in which art was made for private consumption.[10] At the 1870 Salon, Courbet's landscape pair *The Cliffs at Étretat after a Storm* (*La Falaise d'Étretat après l'orage*; 1870, Musée d'Orsay) and *The Wave* (*La Vague*; 1869/70, Alte Nationalgalerie, Berlin) was critically acclaimed and garnered the gold medal, the Salon jury's highest award.

Courbet's triumph occurred within a field of some of the most gifted landscape painters of the day. However, while painters like Charles-François Daubigny and Théodore Rousseau had advanced the aesthetic of naturalistic images emphasizing the artist's immediate perception and his "inner nature" against the stylized rhetorical tradition of the academy, their work remained comparatively marginalized: only in 1867, the year of his death, did Rousseau, the "grande refusée," receive significant official recognition. Camille Corot's landscapes, like those of Rousseau, were brilliantly informed by plein-air practice, but both artists were fairly conservative in their Salon pictures, which were methodically and deliberately completed.[11] Courbet brought not only landscape painting, but specifically the plein-air practice of technical innovation and painterly performance in response to natural phenomenon, to the center of ambitious contemporary production. The young generation of painters in the 1860s, Claude Monet, Camille Pissarro, Auguste Renoir, and above all Paul Cézanne, followed Courbet's lead into a genre defined by its independence and openness to experimentation and personal self-realization. Offering an unrivaled opportunity for artists to improvise within an ever-expanding expressive range of facture, landscape painting would dominate avant-garde practice into the twentieth century.

1. Pierre-Henri de Valenciennes, *Elémens de perspective pratique a l'usage des artistes, suivis de réflexions et conseils à un élève sur la peinture et particulièrement sur le genre du paysage* (Paris: Desenne/Duprat, 1799).

2. For the history of the rediscovery of the plein-air oil sketch tradition, see the introduction to *True to Nature: Open-Air Painting in Europe 1780–1870*, exh. cat. (London: Paul Holberton, 2020), 11–17.

3. Pierre Courthion, ed., *Courbet raconté par lui-même et par ses amis* (Geneva: Pierre Callier, 1948), 197–202. See also Courbet's letter to his family about the episode in *Letters of Gustave Courbet*, ed. and trans. Petra ten-Doesschate Chu (Chicago: University of Chicago Press, 1992), 247.

4. Théophile Thoré, "Salon de 1866," in *Les Salons: Études de critique et d'esthétique* (Brussels: H. Lamertin, 1893), tome 3, 276–80; Bruno Foucart, *G. Courbet* (Naefels: Bonfini, 1977); and Julius Meier-Graefe, *Courbet* (Munich: Piper, 1921). For the values associated with the aesthetic of oil sketching, see Richard R. Brettell, *Impression: Painting Quickly in France 1860–1890*, exh. cat. (New Haven, CT: Yale University Press, 2000).

5. These Naturalist critics included Théophile Thoré, Edmond About, Champfleury, and Jule-Antoine Castagnary.

6. For an excellent and more thorough account of many of the issues sketched in this essay, see Anthea Callen, *The Work of Art: Plein-Air Painting and Artistic Identity in Nineteenth-Century France* (London: Reaktion, 2015).

7. Théophile Silvestre, "Courbet d'après nature," in Courthion, *Courbet raconté par lui-même*, 25–62; Thoré, "Salon de 1861" and "Salon de 1866," in *Les Salons*, tome 2, 36, and tome 3, 276–80; and Comtesse H. D'Ideville, *Gustave Courbet: Notes et documents sur sa vie & son oeuvre*, in Courthion, *Courbet raconté par lui-même*, 213–14.

8. Théodure Duret, *Les Peintres français en 1867* (Paris: E. Dentu, 1867), 85.

9. Nicholas Green, "Dealing in Temperaments: Economic Transformation of the Artistic Field in France during the Second Half of the 19th Century," *Art History* 10, no. 1 (March 1987): 60–61. See also Nicholas Green, *The Spectacle of Nature: Landscape and Bourgeois Culture in Nineteenth-Century France* (Manchester: Manchester University Press, 1990). Green makes the point that the cult of creative individualism centered in landscape painting served the rise of speculative ventures in modern painting. At the heart of this nexus was the dealer Paul Durand-Ruel, who trafficked in plein-air sketches and created a market for Théodore Rousseau's sketches. Durand-Ruel handled Courbet's landscapes as they took off in the early 1870s. See also James Rubin, *Courbet* (London: Phaidon, 1997), 177; Petra ten-Doesschate Chu, *The Most Arrogant Man in France: Gustave Courbet and the Nineteenth-Century Media Culture* (Princeton, NJ: Princeton University Press, 2007); and Petra ten-Doesschate Chu in *Courbet: Artiste et promoteur de son oeuvre*, ed. Jörg Zutter (Paris: Flammarion, 1999), 53–81.

10. Harrison C. White and Cynthia A. White, *Canvases and Careers: Institutional Change in the French Painting World* (Chicago: University of Chicago Press, 1993), 16.

11. Michael F. Zimmerman, "Painting of Nature—Nature of Painting: An Essay on Landscape and the Historical Position of 'Barbizon,'" in *Barbizon: Malerei der Natur—Natur der Malerei*, Andreas Burmester, Christoph H. Heilmann, and Michael F. Zimmerman (Munich: Klinkhardt & Biermann, 1999), 35. On Rousseau, see Greg Thomas, "The Practice of Naturalism: The Working Methods of Théodore Rousseau," in Burmester, Heilmann, and Zimmerman, *Barbizon*, 139; and Scott Allan and Edouard Kopp, *Unruly Nature: The Landscapes of Théodore Rousseau*, exh. cat. (Los Angeles: Getty Publications, 2016). On Corot, see Philip Conisbee, Sarah Faunce, and Jeremy Strick, *In the Light of Italy: Corot and Early Open-Air Painting*, exh. cat. (New Haven, CT: Yale University Press), 1996.

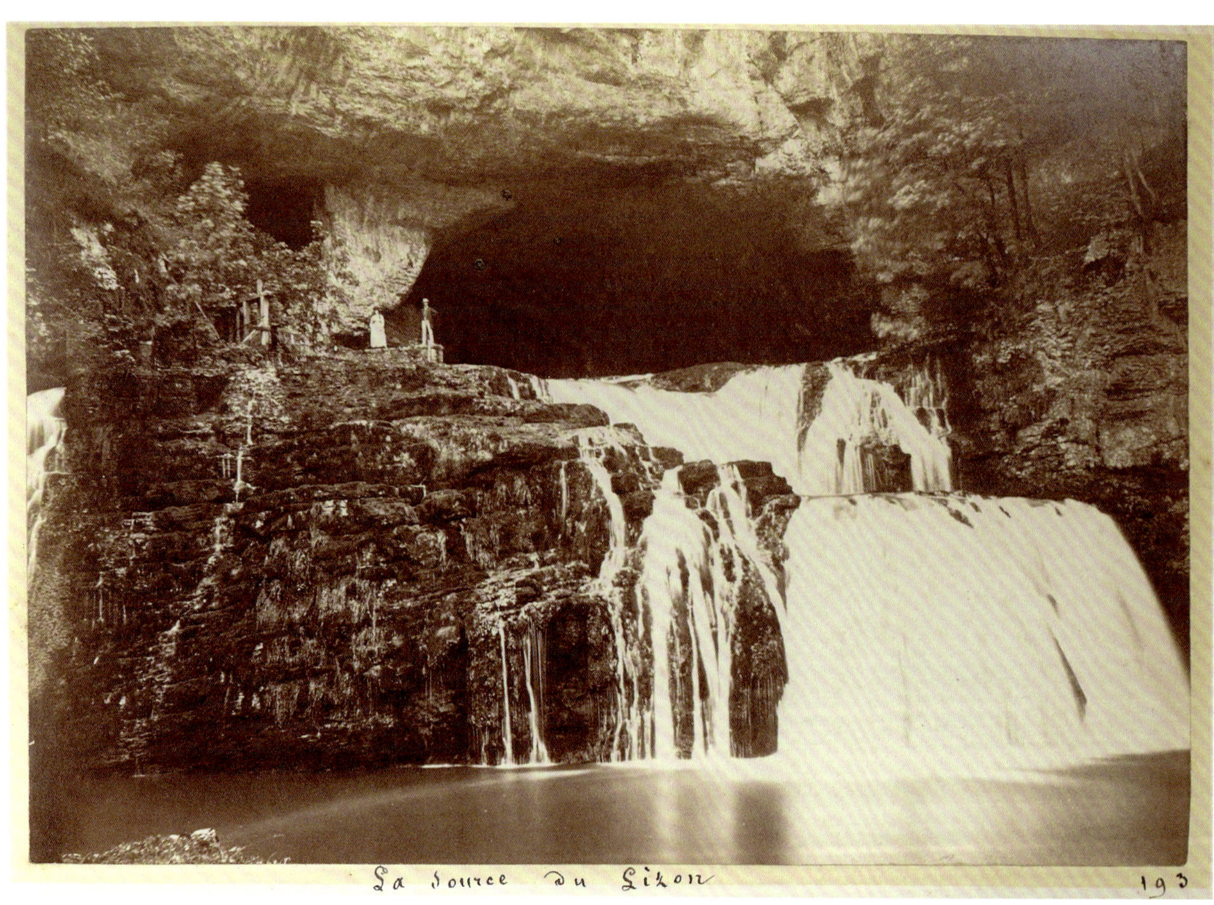

La source du Lizon

193

PATHS TO THE SOURCE:
The Lison and Nineteenth-Century Tourism

JALEN CHANG

Set against the yawning maw of the Lison River's source, two late nineteenth-century *promeneurs*—a woman in white, a man more darkly clad—are the sole, tiny outliers in an otherwise-uninterrupted tableau of natural beauty (**FIG. 6.1**).[1] While it's difficult to say from this distance, they may well be caught in a pose somewhere between spontaneous excitement and comportmental uncertainty, one immediately familiar to anyone who has had their obligatory photograph taken at a sight deemed worth seeing. Despite their ensembles, exceedingly formal in comparison to the athleisure favored by today's hikers, they are closer to our moment than we might realize. During these *promeneurs'* lives, industrialization and urbanization had begun to transform the French countryside into the city's geographic and ideological other, a restorative retreat in which to spend newly demarcated leisure time.[2] Thus, modern ecotourism was born, and photographs like this both testify to and actively whetted a now-widespread, commercialized appetite for travel, the great outdoors, and natural wonders such as the Lison's picturesque origins.

Although they likely did not know it, the *promeneurs'* photograph from their hike that day bears striking similarities to Gustave Courbet's painted representations of the site. Yet, although both views on the source are from almost precisely the same distance and vantage point, an affective gulf remains between keepsake and canvas. To look into the uninhabited depths of the Courbet is, as Paul Galvez has put it, to voyage

FIG. 6.1 Artist unknown, *The Source of the Lison and Two Walkers*, ca. 1875, photographic print, 4 ¾ × 6 ¹¹⁄₁₆ in. (12 × 17 cm). Musée Comtois, Besançon, 2004.00.002.193.

toward "an unknowable point of origin," to ponder primordial geneses of matter—natural and painted alike.[3] In comparison, the question of origins prompted by the photograph is of a more practical nature: How did tourists such as these find their way to that particular spot, perched upon a precarious, slippery rock face about 25 miles south of Besançon and 250 miles southeast of Paris? Hypothetically reconstructing these tourists' journey takes us through histories of print culture, advancements in transportation, and French cultural imaginaries, leading to a place no less revealing about the nineteenth century than Courbet's painterly materialism.[4]

Before our tourists embarked on their getaway, the Lison and the Franche-Comté needed to appear on their radar as a desirable destination. As Petra ten-Doesschate Chu has shown, this was spurred by illustrated travel compendiums like Baron Isidore Justin Taylor and Charles Nodier's *Voyages pittoresques et romantiques dans l'ancienne France*, published from the 1820s through the 1840s. The 1825 iteration dedicated to the Franche-Comté spoke glowingly of both a "people so generous and so constant" and "wonders of a sublime nature," drawing an equivalence between an unspoiled environment and an unspoiled rural people distinct from the cultured armchair travelers who were consulting the tomes.[5] Furthermore, a section titled "The Caves of Osselles" enumerates the region's various speleological attractions, including the Lison's source, described breathlessly in text and depicted in an accompanying lithograph (**FIG. 6.2**).[6] Even in the first quarter of the nineteenth century, the authors of publications such as the *Voyages pittoresque*s were aware that their readers might visit these marvelous sites in person, and thus they were keen to provide practical advice alongside romanticizing paeans. For example, Taylor and Nodier warned readers looking for a place to rest and stay near the Lison to steer clear of the miller, who could not be counted on for clean accommodations. Instead, it would prove worth travelers' time to track down the cottage of the cave caretaker, who could even provide a guide and torches.[7]

FIG. 6.2 James Duffield Harding, *Source of the Lison*, lithograph from Charles Nodier, Isidore-Justin-Séverin Taylor, and Achille-Alexandre-Alphonse de Cailloux de Cailleux, *Voyages pittoresques et romantiques dans l'ancienne France*, vol. 2, *Franche-Comté* (Paris: P. Didot l'aîné, 1825), pl. 116. Cleveland Art Museum: Twenty-fifth anniversary gift, Mr. and Mrs. Lewis B. Williams Collection, 1941.162.

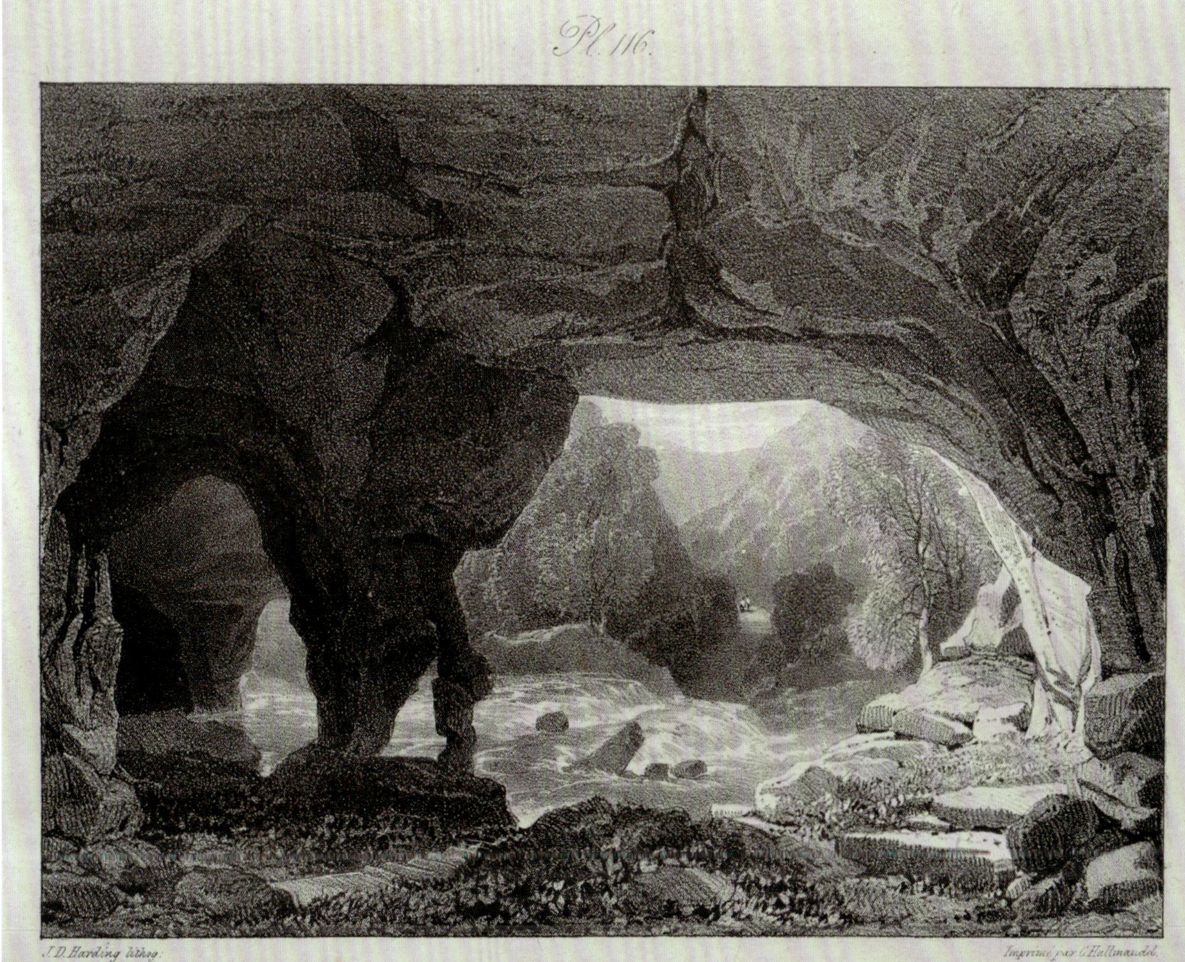

Source du Lison.

Franche Comté.

Once the *promeneurs* had decided on their Franc-comtois sojourn, the next order of business would be to arrange transportation to the region. In the time of the *Voyages pittoresques*, this would almost certainly have been by public stagecoach (*la diligence*). A Parisian passenger, for example, might patronize a *diligence* company that could coordinate all legs of the proposed journey, even those that would eventually require a provincial coach operator. One could select a class of seat, negotiate a luggage allowance, and prepay per league to be traveled. However, despite the mental relief of a trip settled from start to finish, *diligences* were less convenient when the wood hit the road. *Murray's Handbook for Travellers in France*, a popular English travel guide, described the coach as a "huge, heavy, lofty, lumbering machine" that could reach six or seven miles per hour only in the most pristine weather conditions.[8]

FIG. 6.3 A. M. Perrot, *Département du Doubs*, engraved by E. Grezel and Ch. Smith, from Victor Levasseur, *Atlas national illustré: Region de l'est* (Paris: A. Combette, 1856), no. 24. David Rumsey Historical Map Collection, Stanford University.

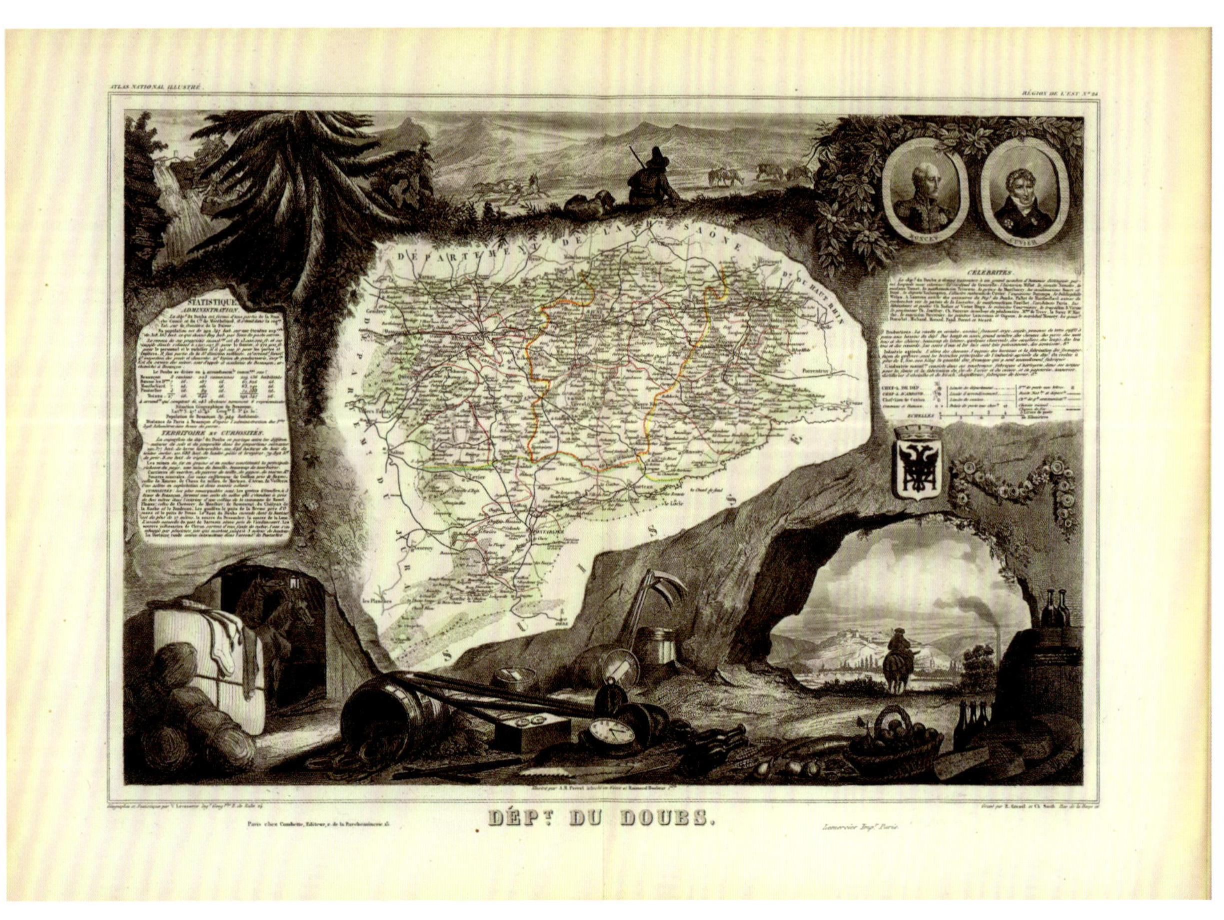

Thankfully for our 1870s *promeneurs'* comfort in transit, it is far more likely that they arrived in the Franche-Comté by train. Less than a decade before Courbet painted the Lison's source in 1864, train stations opened in Besançon and Salins, connecting the region to the national rail network, which had been rapidly branching outward from Paris since 1842.[9] An 1856 illustrated map of Doubs even depicts the new rail line running through Besançon, along with lists of famous natives of the region, local economic products, and notable natural sights including the Loue River's source (**FIG. 6.3**). The ever-expanding transit system was a massive boon to the budding tourist industry, and travel guides were quick to adjust to the newly dominant mode of transport. The renowned Richard's *Guide du voyageur en France*— regularly updated since 1815—reworked its entire structure in the late 1840s to revolve around the existing lines, detailing connections, fares, and possible day trips from each stop, no matter how remote.[10] In the 1866 edition, the *Guide* proposed a hike from the small village of Nans-sous-Sainte-Anne, easily reached by route 38 from Paris to Salins. The centerpiece of the day would be a stop at the Lison's source, accessible with some effort from a "winding path" concealed at "the base of a rock wall." The Richard guide's specificity does not halt at the cave's threshold; intrepid travelers are encouraged to enter the grotto and discover a peculiar rock formation dubbed "the preacher's pulpit" by the locals. The entire trip, which included other notable natural sights in the region, could be completed on foot in eight hours—the same duration of the train from Paris to Salins, the closest rail stop to Nans-sous-Sainte-Anne.[11]

In under twenty-four (exhausting) hours, our *promeneurs* could have left Paris and feasibly placed themselves into the very Lison tableau they had seen in the *Voyages pittoresques* earlier that day. Afterward, the tourists could have indulged post-hike at the thermal baths of Salins-les-Bains, patronized the celebrated watchmakers of Besançon, or visited the alleged ancient battle site of Alesia, all attractions suggested by period guidebooks to

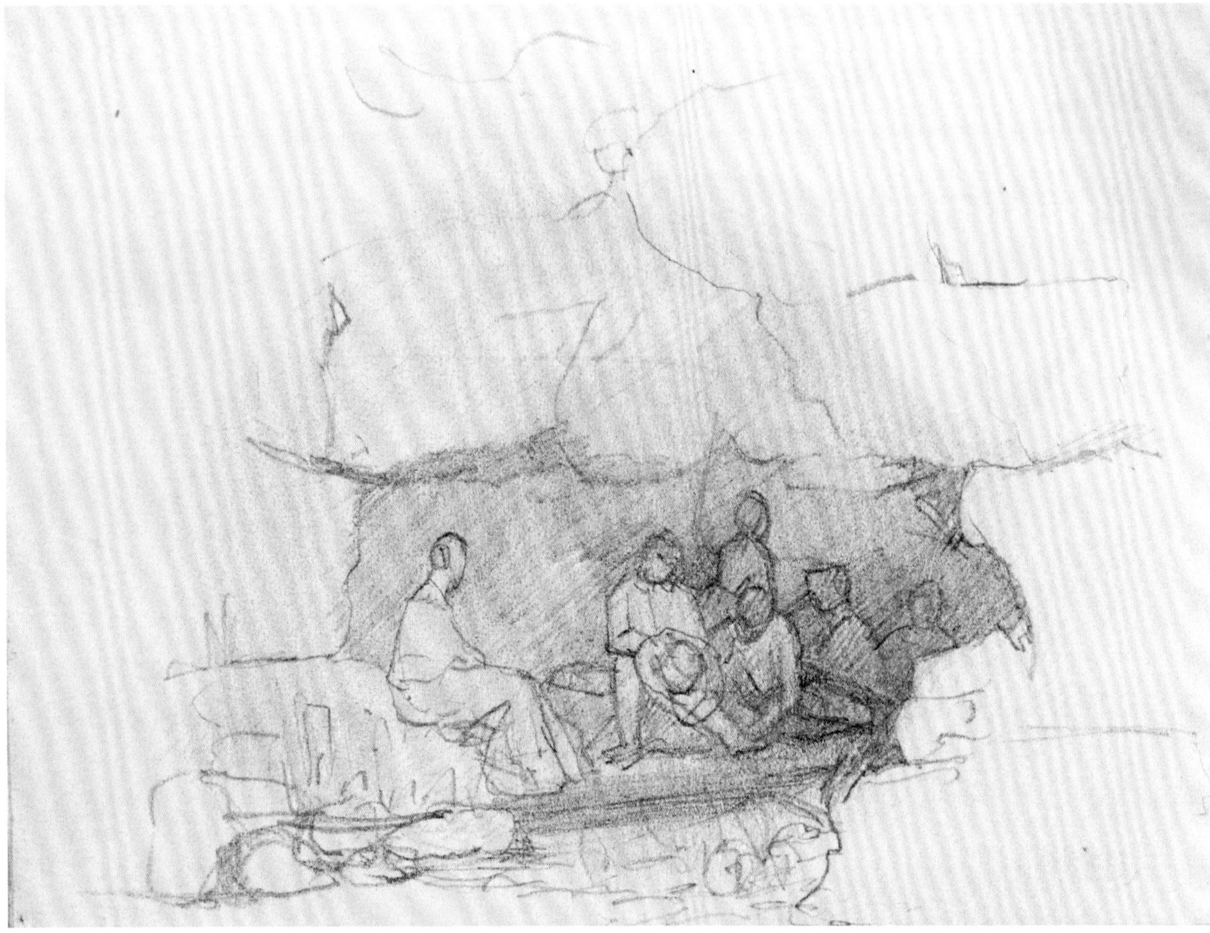

the Franche-Comté.[12] Despite its sublime grandeur and imposing cascades, the Lison's source was but a single point in the compressed matrix of time and distance created by nineteenth-century modernization and tourism. Of course, Courbet was aware of the Lison's wider popularity. An 1840s sketchbook page shows hikers, much like those in our photograph, briefly resting while exploring a local cave (**FIG. 6.4**). Thus, our *promeneurs'* hypothetical journey to the river's source can lend us a new perspective on the formal particularities of Courbet's Lison pictures—durational, decelerated, individuated experiences more akin to the "winding path" described by Richard than to the crowded line from Paris to Salins.

FIG. 6.4 Gustave Courbet, *Hikers Resting in a Rock Shelter*, early 1840s, graphite on paper, sketchbook page, fol. 24 verso, 3 15/16 × 5 5/16 in. (10.1 × 13.6 cm). Musée du Louvre, RF 9105, 45.

1. *Randonneurs*, the present-day word for "hikers," did not come into widespread use until the twentieth century.

2. Nicholas Green, *The Spectacle of Nature: Landscape and Bourgeois Culture in Nineteenth-Century France* (Manchester: Manchester University Press, 1990), 80–84.

3. Paul Galvez, *Courbet's Landscapes: The Origins of Modern Painting* (New Haven, CT: Yale University Press, 2022), 81.

4. Petra Chu's work on Courbet's landscape marketing strategy and awareness of tourists' taste deeply informs this essay. See Petra ten-Doesschate Chu, "The Purposeful Sightseer: Courbet and Mid-Nineteenth-Century Tourism," in *Looking at the Landscapes: Courbet and Modernism. Papers from a Symposium Held at the J. Paul Getty Museum on March 18, 2006*, ed. Mary Morton (Los Angeles: J. Paul Getty Museum, 2007), https://www.getty.edu/publications/virtuallibrary/0892369272.html?imprint=jpgt; and Petra ten-Doesschate Chu, "It Took Millions of Years to Compose That Picture," in *Courbet Reconsidered*, ed. Sarah Faunce and Linda Nochlin, exh. cat. (New Haven, CT: Yale University Press, 1988), 55–66.

5. Charles Nodier, Justin Taylor, and Alphonse Cailleux, *Voyages pittoresques et romantiques dans l'ancienne France*, vol. 2, *Franche-Comté* (Paris: J. Didot l'aîné, 1825), 8, 10, trans. by the author.

6. Nodier, Taylor, and Cailleux, *Voyages pittoresques*, 163.

7. Nodier, Taylor, and Cailleux, 158n1.

8. *Murray's Handbook for Travellers in France* (London: John Murray, 1858), xxvi.

9. Jean Cuynet, *Histoire du rail en Franche-Comté* (Nice: La Régordane, 1989).

10. On the aesthetic conventions of such guidebooks and their influences on the French landscape tradition, see Greg M. Thomas, "The Topographical Aesthetic in French Tourism and Landscape," *Nineteenth-Century Art Worldwide* 1, no. 1 (Spring 2002): http://www.19thc-artworldwide.org/spring02/198-the-topographical-aesthetic-in-french-tourism-and-landscape.

11. Jean-Marie-Vincent Audin (pseudonym Richard), *Guide du voyageur en France*, 26th edition (Paris: Hachette, 1866), 120–22.

12. Alphonse Delacroix, *Guide de l'étranger à Besançon et en Franche-Comté: Accompagné d'une carte du siège d'Alesia* (Besançon: Bulle, 1860).

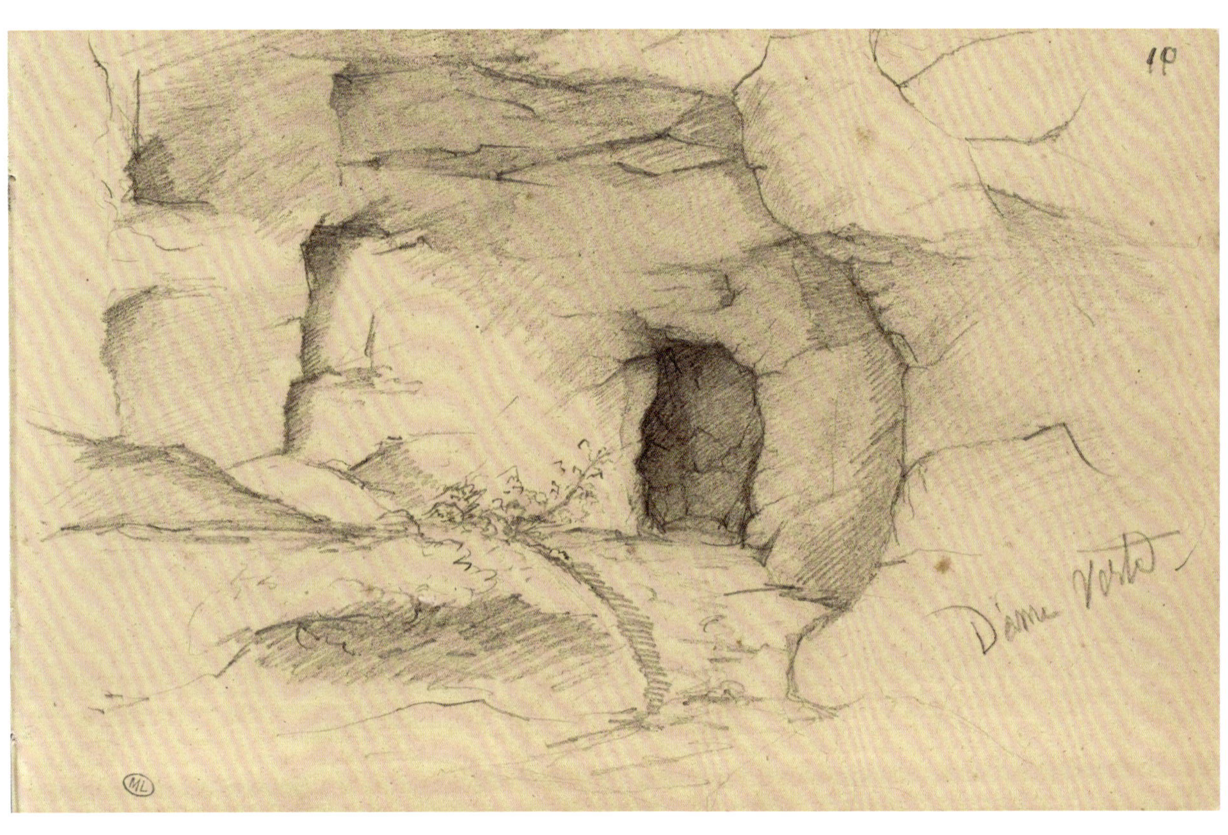
19
Dôme Vert
ML

SOURCE, ORIGIN, ENDPOINT, PROJECTION, POSSESSION

ARUNA D'SOUZA

One of the most persistent readings of Gustave Courbet's images of sources and grottoes—geological sites dotting the Franche-Comté landscape that he painted repeatedly in the mid-1860s—aligns their shadowed outcroppings of rock, scrubby foliage, and deep, dark caves and chasms with the sexual anatomy of the woman's body.[1] This interpretation was perhaps encouraged by the fact that grottoes in the Jura were referred to by locals as "ladies," and regional folklore regarded them as the home of fairies, nymphs, and other, perhaps more dangerous, mythical feminine beings.[2] Even more telling, Werner Hofmann notes, is the presence in one of Courbet's early sketchbooks of a drawing depicting a cave on which the artist has handwritten a title, "Dame Verte" (Green Lady; **FIG. 7.1**).[3] In large part, this landscape-body link has led commentators on the artist's work to understand his fascination with such scenes as rooted in a fundamentally libidinal impulse, a tendency summed up by Dominique de Font-Réaulx's description of the way the paintings demonstrate an "intimate knowledge of the places represented, with a strong, carnal, loving union between the artist and the valleys where he grew up."[4] Michael Fried goes so far as to refer to the landscapes as "a subgroup of Courbet's paintings of women," while Paul Galvez refers to their particular spatial constructions as "initiating an invagination of space."[5]

This approach to Courbet's Source of the Loue (**FIG. 7.2**) and Source of the Lison paintings (see figs. 1.1, 1.2)—one that will presumably adhere to the rediscovered iteration of the

FIG. 7.1 Gustave Courbet, *Rocky Landscape*, inscribed "Dame Verte," n.d., graphite on paper, sketchbook page, fol. 10 recto, 5 ½ × 8 ⁹⁄₁₆ in. (14 × 21.7 cm). Musée du Louvre, RF29234, 17.

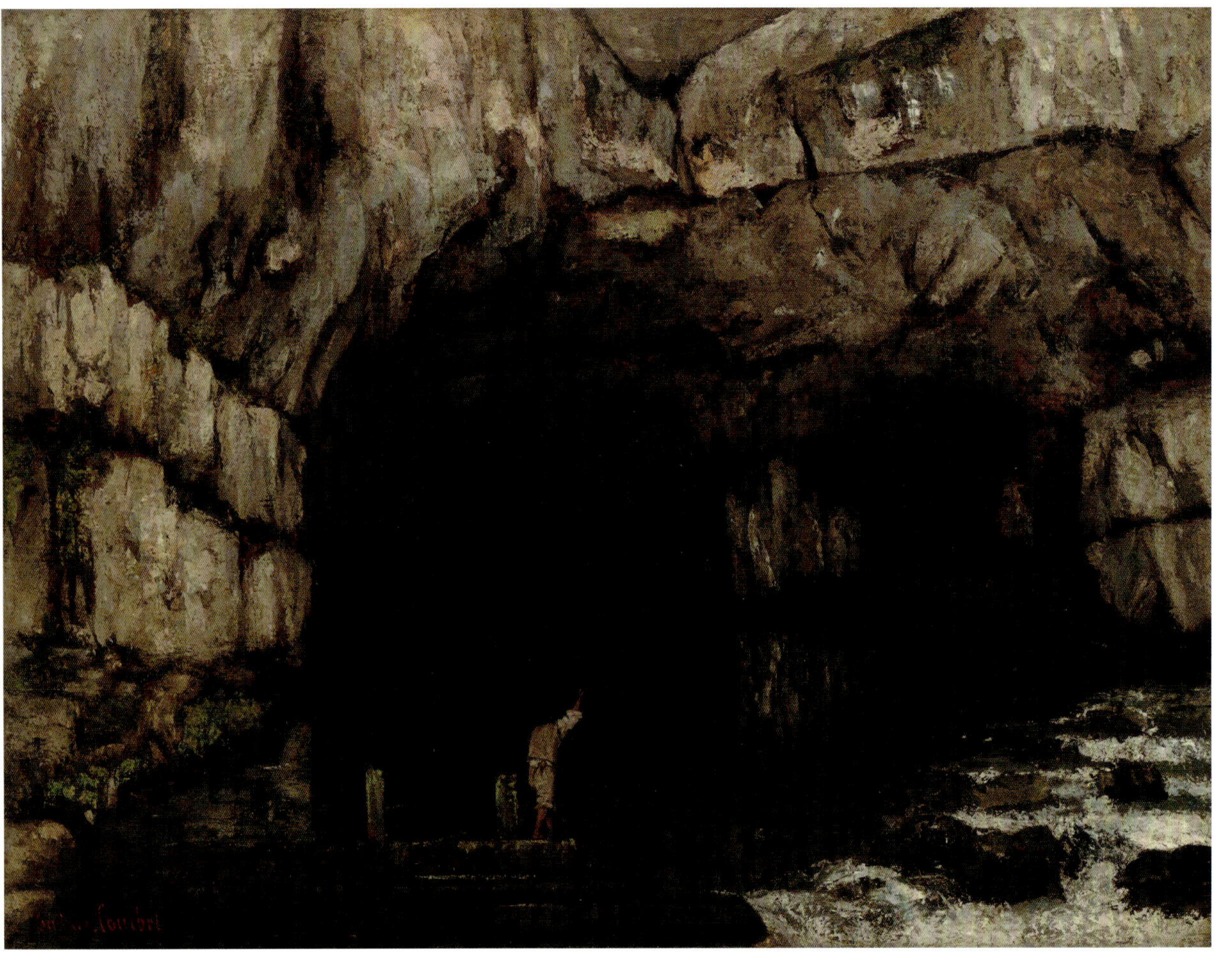

latter motif at the University of Pennsylvania—predated the
unearthing of the artist's infamous painting *The Origin of the World*
(*L'Origine du monde*; **FIG. 7.3**). This work, a bodily topography
of parted thighs, pubic mound, and partial torso, was painted
in 1866 but secreted away in private collections until it was
unearthed by Linda Nochlin and Sarah Faunce for their 1988
exhibition *Courbet Reconsidered*.[6] The reentry of *Origin* into the
Courbet canon was thus at most an apparent *confirmation* of
what many had already proposed, as Nochlin noted in a 1986
article about the pair's search for the lost canvas: "The reading
of landscape as a manifestation of the psychoanalytic process of
displacement in Courbet's oeuvre becomes even clearer if
we consider a work like *The Source of the Loue*—itself the
representation of an origin, or source—whose morphological

FIG. **7.2** Gustave Courbet, *La Grotte de la Loue,*
1864, oil on canvas, 38 ¾ × 51 ⁵⁄₁₆ in. (98.4 × 130.4
cm). National Gallery of Art, Washington, DC,
Gift of Charles L. Lindemann, 1957.6.1.

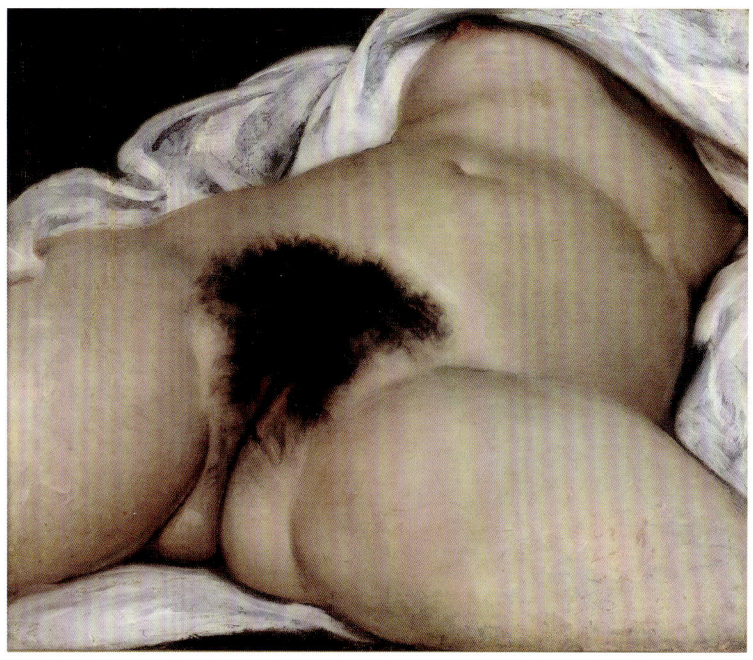

relationship to *The Origin of the World* has often been asserted in the Courbet literature."[7] Font-Réaulx makes a very direct comparison when she writes that "the works have a similar theme, that of a universal source, an original womb; a similar composition, the thighs of the woman forming two cliffs between which the grotto opens up; a similar palette blending ochres, browns, reds, and greys; and paint applied in a powerful manner, with large movements of the knife."[8]

The seemingly obvious relationship between *Origin* and Courbet's various scenes of sources and grottoes has been claimed so often that one might say that if *The Origin of the World* did not exist, art history would have had to invent it, if only to justify the fact that a sexualized, gendered, even libidinal reading of Courbet's landscapes has existed almost from the beginning of the artist's career. His shocking nude likely had many birthplaces—including an ongoing rivalry with Édouard Manet, a leading artist of the 1860s Parisian avant-garde whose urbane coolness, embodied in works like *Olympia* (1863, Musée d'Orsay, Paris), was threatening Courbet's position in the art world.[9] Yet it does seem, too, that the work functioned as a literalization, or a logical outcome, of an approach to image making that Courbet had turned into a "personal brand" (to use an anachronistic term) over the years.

The analogy between Courbet's Source paintings and *Origin* has largely been made on the basis of the analogy between the vagina as a kind of cave or grotto and what Laurence des Cars calls, in her description of Courbet's "ultra-feminized landscapes," the "irresistibly attractive and frightening darkness" at the heart of the pictures.[10] But what has always struck me as odd about this comparison is that it doesn't align—at all—with what one actually sees in *Origin*. No caves—or vaginas—here: instead of inky shadows and unplumbed depths we see a fluffy mound of pubic hair, a barely open vulval slit, a hint of labial fold, and beyond that, beautifully painted expanses of bare belly and thigh and breast. The "hole"—itself an entirely heterosexist understanding of what the vagina is when it's not being penetrated by a penis, but an understanding on which so many art historical analyses depend nonetheless—is nowhere visible.

With this in mind, it is perhaps more correct to say that rather than translating the anatomy of a woman's body into the geological and topographical terms of painting, Courbet's pictures of sources and grottoes show us what is, in fact, anatomically hidden from view. They lay bare what cannot be seen without a speculum—becoming, as Nochlin argues in her gloss on *Origin*, a site of displacement of Courbet's masculine fears of female sexuality. The landscapes say, that is, what even a painting as almost unimaginably frank as *Origin* cannot. As Ulf Küster puts it, the grottoes "might well be metaphors not so much of the vulva as of the abysses of sexuality, which cannot be depicted as such."[11]

One might turn to the art critic, journalist, and sometime-politician Jules-Antoine Castagnary for a slightly less anatomical, though undoubtedly sexualized, reading of Courbet's landscapes. In 1882, he wrote:

[Courbet] discovered virgin lands where no one had yet placed a foot, aspects and forms of landscape that one could say were unknown before he painted them. . . . Each time he

plunged into the bosom of deep nature, he was like a man
who has penetrated a beehive and come out covered in honey;
he returned charged with perfume and poetry. He descended
into the deep irregular hollows where the spring is born of
the trickle from rocks, he watched the drops of water collect,
let slide between his fingers the silver of small waterfalls.
. . . No one painted in strokes so frank, just that quivering
humidity.[12]

By the time Castagnary wrote these lines—lines, it must
be said, that convey the same heated, erotic Romanticism of
something like Samuel Taylor Coleridge's 1816 poem "Kublai
Khan," which is a thinly veiled description of a woman's body in
terms of landscape—he had already seen *Origin* in Halil Şerif
Bey's private chambers.[13] But even so, he is not seduced into being
sidetracked by caves and hidden depths. Instead, Castagnary's
language focuses on Courbet's pleasure in the engagement with
his subject matter: he discovers virgin lands, he plunges into
bosoms, he delves into hollows, he gets covered in sweet nectar,
he is reenergized, and so on. He revels in the landscape the way he
might revel in a woman's body, but the focus is less the body than
the reveling.

And this is the point, isn't it: ultimately, no less than *The
Origin of the World* itself, Courbet's *Source of the Loue* and his
other paintings of these sorts of sites are less about women (even
merely women reduced to their anatomical parts) than they are
about men and their imaginings. And they are, likewise, about
possession, power, mastery, and control. As Mary Morton notes,
the contemporary interpretation of Courbet's landscapes was
bound up with the artist's performance of masculinity, as images
expressing "a masculine vitality with undercurrents of violence,"
made with a palette knife rather than a brush, "a brutal weapon
. . . evoking images of the artist attacking his paint surface."[14]
Along with his deliberately coarse, countrified ways and his
rejection of codes of bourgeois behavior—behavior he deemed
"effete"—the immediacy, seemingly rough paint application,

immersive points of view, and untamed wildernesses that characterized his scenes of the Franche-Comté seemed to underline his machismo. He embodied a painterly gaze, one might say, in which the possession of women—and of space itself—was merely an extension of his attitude toward the world. To see in Courbet's Source paintings an echo of *The Origin of the World* is to make manifest or to make obvious this gendered gaze, a gaze that operates in Courbet's work regardless of genre or subject matter.

In 2013, after a bout of serious illness, my teacher and friend Linda Nochlin asked me to accompany her on a trip to Ornans, so that she could visit one last time the sites that had become so familiar to her over the course of a lifetime studying Courbet. Despite her frailty, Linda—whose athleticism was always a point of pride—insisted on taking a long walk down to the source of the Loue. When we got there, she was reenergized, as if this place were indeed a source of life, or at least liveliness. This paper is dedicated to her—to the person who is, to me, a source and an origin, and a treasured and much-missed interlocutor about all things Courbet.

1. Here, and throughout this paper, I refer to cis women's bodies, with the understanding that there are other types of bodies that also possess vulvas and vaginas, and that not all women's bodies do either.
2. Ulf Küster, "Gustave Courbet, Avant-Garde Artist," in *Gustave Courbet*, ed. Ulf Küster, exh. cat. (Ostfildern: Hatje Cantz, 2014), 17–18.
3. Werner Hofmann, "Courbets Wirklichkeiten," in *Courbet und Deutschland*, ed. Werner Hofmann and Klaus Herding, exh. cat. (Cologne: DuMont, 1978), 590–613.
4. Dominique de Font-Réaulx, "Reproducing Reality: Landscape Photography of the 1850s and 1860s in Relation to the Paintings of Gustave Courbet," in *Courbet and the Modern Landscape*, ed. Mary Morton and Charlotte Eyerman, exh. cat. (Los Angeles: Getty Museum, 2006), 39.
5. Michael Fried, *Courbet's Realism* (Chicago: University of Chicago Press, 1992), 209. Paul Galvez, "Painting at the Origin," in *Looking at the Landscapes: Courbet and Modernism. Papers from a Symposium Held at the J. Paul Getty Museum on March 8, 2006*, ed. Mary Morton (Los Angeles: Getty Publications, 2007), 50, https://www.getty.edu /publications/resources /virtuallibrary/0892369272.pdf.
6. *The Origin of the World* was painted as part of a commission for Halil Şerif Bey, commonly referred to in Paris as Khalil Bey, an Egyptian serving in the Ottoman diplomatic service. While it remained in private collections until 1995, when it entered the Musée d'Orsay, it was known to have existed thanks to contemporary accounts by those who claimed to have been given access to it in Bey's private apartments. A black-and-white photograph of the painting was reproduced in 1930 in a book titled *Die grossen Meister der Erotik* by Eduard Fuchs. A colored photograph of the painting emerged in Gérard Zwang's 1967 book *Le Sexe de la femme*, but this turned out not to be a reproduction of the Courbet original—it was, in fact, a photo of a 1940 "replica" of the original made by René Magritte using only the black-and-white photo as guidance. See Linda Nochlin, "Courbet's *L'Origine du monde*: The Origin without an Original," *October* 37 (Summer 1986): 76–86; reprinted in Linda Nochlin, *Courbet* (New York: Thames & Hudson, 2007), 145–52. For a full accounting of the painting's provenance, see Thierry Savatier, *L'Origine du Monde: Histoire d'un tableau de Gustave Courbet*, 2nd ed. (Paris: Bartillat, 2006); and Frédérique Thomas-Maurin, Julie Delmas, and Élise Boudon, *Cet obscur objet des désirs: Autour de 'L'Origine du Monde,'* exh. cat. (Ornans: Musée Gustave Courbet, 2014).
7. Linda Nochlin, "Courbet's *L'Origine du monde*," in *Courbet*, 149. Nochlin refers here to the version at the National Gallery of Art in Washington, DC. Laurence Madeline notes that whatever Courbet's psychoanalytic reasons for drawing such an analogy, the "genitals-as-grotto metaphor" was frequent in erotic literature of the time. See Laurence Madeline, "The Origin of the World," in Küster, *Gustave Courbet*, 139.
8. Font-Réaulx, "Reproducing Reality," 45–46.
9. On this point, see Nanette Solomon, "Courbet's *Woman with a Parrot* and

the Problem of 'Realism,'" in *Tribute to Lotte Brand Philip: Art Historian and Detective*, ed. William W. Clark (New York: Abaris, 1985), 144–53; and Laurence des Cars, "A Legacy of Truth: The Reference to Courbet from Manet to Cézanne," in *Gustave Courbet*, ed. Dominique de Font-Réaulx, exh. cat. (New York: Metropolitan Museum of Art, 2008), 59–69.

10. Laurence des Cars, "Courbet the Landscapist," in Font-Réaulx, *Gustave Courbet*, 268.

11. Küster, "Gustave Courbet, Avant-Garde Artist," 18.

12. Jules-Antoine Castagnary, *Exposition des oeuvres de Gustave Courbet: À l'École des Beaux-Arts* (Paris: Émile Martinet, 1882), 17–18, quoted in Mary Morton, "To Create a Living Art: Rethinking Courbet's Landscape Painting," in Morton and Eyerman, *Courbet and the Modern Landscape*, 9.

13. In fact, Castagnary had written a poem about *Origin* as well; the scholar Thierry Savatier found the manuscript in his papers. My research—the subject of a forthcoming publication— indicates that far from being a private meditation on the work, the poem was published widely at the time of its writing.

14. Morton, "To Create a Living Art," 9. For an extensive discussion of Courbet's self-fashioning vis-à-vis the rapidly changing art market of the era, see Petra ten-Doesschate Chu, *The Most Arrogant Man in France: Gustave Courbet and the Nineteenth-Century Media Culture* (Princeton, NJ: Princeton University Press, 2007).

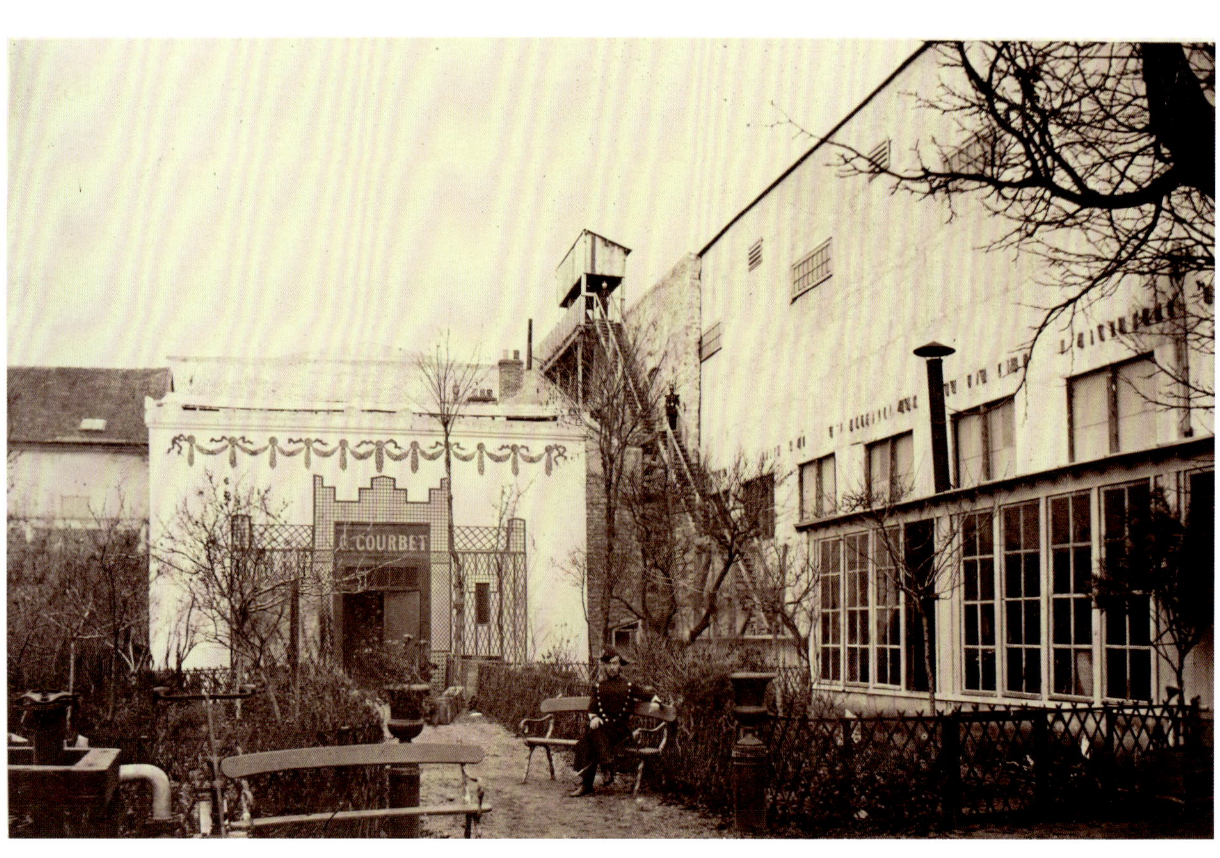
G. COURBET

DISPLAYS OF POWER:
Courbet as Exhibition Maker

EMILY ZIMMERMAN

The period in which Gustave Courbet painted *The Source of the Lison* (*La Source du Lison*; see fig. 1.1) is bookended by two major and unprecedented endeavors that considered a different kind of landscape: the gallery wall. In 1855 and 1867, Courbet independently organized exhibitions of his work outside of the official Salon: his famous Pavilion of Realism (Pavillon du réalisme; **FIG. 8.1**) and his pavilion outside the 1867 Exposition Universelle in Paris. These two exhibitions would become the catalyst for the unraveling of salon-style hanging, marking a turn in the spatial logic by which exhibitions were organized. Histories of exhibitions and curatorial practice have widely credited Courbet's Pavilion of Realism with introducing modernism in the display of artwork, from Brian O'Doherty's *Inside the White Cube* to Bruce Altshuler's *Exhibitions That Made Art History* and Elena Filipovic's anthology *The Artist as Curator*.[1] "In a time long before the advent of the fully professionalized species known as the 'curator,'" Filiopvic points out, "an artist was endeavoring on his own, to choose the location, organize the scenography, make the selection of artworks to be featured, and even devising a financial scheme—all so that he might better determine the conditions of his work's reception."[2]

Mounting these two exhibitions was not merely a self-serving act for Courbet; it was also entwined with the artist's larger project of social critique that resisted the authority of the Salon, the Académie des Beaux-Arts, and Napoléon III. As O'Doherty and others have written, the spatial logic of an exhibition is a

FIG. 8.1 Charles Thurston Thompson, *Fireman's Station. Paris Universal Exhibition*, 1855, albumen print. Victoria and Albert Museum, 33391. The entrance to Courbet's Pavilion of Realism is visible in the background.

manifestation of social, economic, and political ideologies, and the practice of salon-style hanging was a spatialization of the social hierarchy that dominated French life. Over the decade leading up to the 1855 Exposition Universelle, Courbet worked on a large-scale canvas that also served as an allegory of French social life and political power, originally titled *The Painter's Studio: A Real Allegory Summing Up Seven Years of My Artistic and Moral Life* (*L'Atelier du peintre, allégorie réelle déterminant une phase de sept années de ma vie artistique;* see fig. 5.4). While produced specifically for the Salon at the 1855 exposition,[3] the canvas sets aside the rules of academic composition to chart a set of relations between the figures depicted: Courbet at its center, painting a landscape of the Franche-Comté, surrounded by friends and patrons on one side and figures from French, Polish, Russian, and Italian political life on the other. Linda Nochlin summarily argues of the painting, "In the Carnival atmosphere created by the Paris World's Fair, Courbet it would seem, felt free—indeed called upon—to reverse the 'normal' order of the world. . . . In hiding politically subversive meanings under the cloak of allegory, *The Painter's Studio* looks back at a time-honored tradition connecting the rhetorical mode with political subterfuge."[4] Courbet's contemporaneous Pavilion of Realism aligns with this endeavor to intervene in a system of power.

Thwarting Courbet's plan to show *The Painter's Studio* in the French section of the painting exhibition of the 1855 Exposition Universelle, the committee rejected the painting, while accepting eleven of his other artworks, including landscapes such as *Rock of Ten Hours* (*La Roche de Dix Heures*) from 1854 (Musée d'Orsay, Paris), and *The Stream* (*Le Ruisseau du Puits-noir; Vallée de la Loue*) from 1855 (National Gallery of Art, Washington, DC). Rather than acquiesce to their decision, Courbet created his Pavilion of Realism on June 28, 1855, across the street from the main venue, a plan he laid out in an 1854 letter to Alfred Bruyas.[5] Courbet's biographer Jules-Antoine Castagnary later summarized this act of rebellion: "At this time he profited by the occasion offered to him by the world's fair to take the public opinion to task. At his own expense he constructed, in the avenue Montaigne, a sort of barrack in which he installed his collected oeuvre: forty paintings and four drawings."[6] The exhibition included *The Painters's Studio*, *A Burial at Ornans* (*Un enterrement à Ornans*; 1849–50, Musée d'Orsay), *Young Ladies of the Village* (*Les Demoiselles de village*; 1851–52, Metropolitan Museum of Art, New York), and others. Courbet's landscape paintings from this time were included among the eleven paintings shown in the 1855 Exposition Universelle, as landscape was one of the categories accepted by the Salon.

The works in the Pavilion of Realism were not hung salon style; rather, Courbet included more space between the artworks, "in the English style," as the art critic Champfleury wrote to George Sand in 1855.[7] The Académie des Beaux-Arts worked to reaffirm French national identity by separating itself from rival states such as England—and from the vicissitudes of commerce.[8] Courbet's riposte, in its appropriation of the hanging style of English commercial galleries, was thus twofold. He incorporated commerce into the exhibition at numerous junctures: he charged an admission of 1 franc at the door, hosted a paid coat-check, sold a catalogue (with the heading "Exhibition and Sale"), which included his "Realist Manifesto" and cost 10 centimes, advertised the exhibition in the local paper, and offered the artwork for sale. His Pavilion of Realism did not do well, but it received a significant amount of press attention and established Courbet's reputation as an enfant terrible. The 1867 Exposition Universelle featured independent exhibitions by both Courbet (**FIG. 8.2**) and his rival Édouard Manet at the Rond-Point de l'Alma, again just outside the fairgrounds. Courbet included over one hundred works by a range of artists across all genres, as well as several of his own, such as *The Source of the Loue* (*La Grotte de la Loue*; see fig. 7.2). As opposed to his 1855 exhibition, the 1867 one was well attended and positively received. Castagnary tells the story of a visit to the exhibition by Adolphe Thiers (the future president of the Third Republic), who responded to the exhibition: "He loves truth too much, one should not love truth to such an extent."[9]

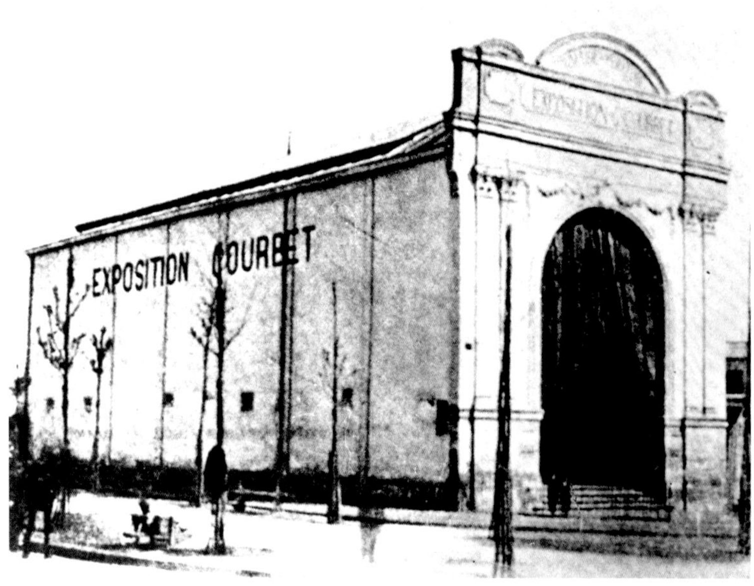

FIG. 8.2 Courbet exhibition at the Rond-Point de l'Alma in Paris, 1867.

It is no mistake that Courbet chose to stage both of his independent pavilions to coincide with world's fairs in Paris, an exhibition that claimed to render the world visible, and that acted as a tool to align subjects with the ideology of empire.[10] Sitting just outside the bounds of these state-crafted displays of power, Courbet's independent exhibitions offered the fairs' 15 million visitors a contrasting model of display. Courbet's work as a curator and his landscape painting may have shared similar goals: to articulate a critique of power structures under the repression of the Second Empire. Painting the Franche-Comté during the high tide of industrial revolution in Paris offered a way of valorizing that which remained unconquerable and untamed. According to the scholar Klaus Herding, Courbet's landscapes have been tied to his social critique of the French government, as in the landscape that appears in *The Painter's Studio*, in which "unspoiled nature was meant to represent freedom from Napoleonic oppression."[11] Mounted immediately before and after Courbet produced this body of landscape work—particularly the Source paintings from the Franche-Comté—these two radical curatorial gestures likewise acted as a contest to state power. Yet they would have lasting effects in the realm of curating, changing the ideological ground—the wall itself—upon which artworks were displayed. This prying open of space between paintings would open up the gallery wall to be the support for a different set of values over the next century. Today, when the repressive colonialist values undergirding museums and the white-cube model of display are under interrogation, it is important to return to Courbet's intervention into the exhibition practices of his day to understand the way that power is wielded through display.

1. Brian O'Doherty, in *Inside the White Cube*, famously cites Courbet as organizing the first modern exhibition, declaring his "one-man Salon des Refuses [*sic*] outside the Exposition of 1855 . . . the first time a modern artist (who happened to be the first modern artist) had to construct the context of his work and therefore editorialize about its values." Brian O'Doherty, *Inside the White Cube* (San Francisco: Lapsis, 1986), 24. See also Bruce Altshuler, *Salon to Biennial: Exhibitions That Made Art History*, vol. 1, *1863–1959* (London: Phaidon, 2008); and Elena Filipovic, ed., *The Artist as Curator* (Milan: Mousse, 2017).

2. Elena Filipovic, "Introduction," in Filipovic, *Artist as Curator*, 7.

3. As Linda Nochlin notes, Courbet's painting was destined for "an exhibition designed to enable France to display her technological prowess and cultural achievement to the world in competition, primarily, with its archival, England." Linda Nochlin, "The Painter's Studio," in *Courbet* (New York: Thames & Hudson, 2007), 183.

4. Nochlin, "Painter's Studio," 182.

5. Courbet wrote to Alfred Bruyas: "Terrible things have happened to me. They just refused my *Burial* and my last picture the *Atelier* as well as the portrait of Champfleury. They declared it was necessary at any cost to arrest the progress of my movement which had a disastrous effect on French art." Quoted in Margaret Armbrust Seibert, "A Political and Pictorial Tradition Used in Gustave Courbet's *Real Allegory*," *Art Bulletin* 65, no. 2 (June 1983): 311.

6. Jules-Antoine Castagnary, "A Biography of Courbet," in *Courbet in Perspective*, ed. Petra ten-Doesschate Chu (Englewood Cliffs, NJ: Prentice-Hall, 1977), 16–17.

7. Champfleury [Jules François Felix Fleury-Husson] to George Sand, September 1855, reproduced in Linda Nochlin, *Realism and Tradition in Art, 1848–1900* (Englewood Cliffs, NJ: Prentice-Hall, 1966), 42.

8. "Hostility to commerce was a significant feature of the ideological ground of the Academy, whose members served the state through the elevated practice of history painting." Linda Nochlin, "Painter's Studio," 181.

9. Castagnary, "Biography of Courbet," 21.

10. André Dombrowski, "Introduction: The World on View," in *The World on View: Objects from Universal Expositions, 1851–1915*, ed. André Dombrowski, exh. cat. (Philadelphia: Department of the History of Art, University of Pennsylvania, 2018), 11.

11. Klaus Herding, *Courbet: To Venture Independence*, trans. John William Gabriel (New Haven, CT: Yale University Press, 1991), 77.

COURBET, OR NOT COURBET, THAT IS THE QUESTION

PETRA TEN-DOESSCHATE CHU

INTRODUCTION

While problems of attribution are common to many nineteenth-century French painters, Gustave Courbet is a champion in the arena of dubious authenticity. Even during his lifetime, the market was flooded with outright forgeries as well as with works by his students and followers to which unscrupulous dealers had added Courbet's signature or initials. The problem is especially thorny for the artist's late landscapes and still lifes. Because few of Courbet's paintings of the last six years of his life can be attributed to him with absolute certainty, there is no adequate body of work that can serve as a benchmark. Thus, connoisseurs are forced to compare works of the seventies with those of the sixties, without truly understanding the evolution that took place in the artist's painting style during the final years of his career. What complicates matters further is Courbet's known practice of making copies or pastiches of his own paintings, sometimes years after he had first painted them. This makes it all the more difficult to trace a clear path of the artist's stylistic development.

Readers who expect to find in this article a recipe for separating true from false in the body of work attributed to Courbet will be disappointed. Such a recipe, unfortunately, does not exist. Instead, the purpose of this article is to highlight the authentication problems presented by Courbet's paintings, especially the late ones, and to ground them in their historical context.[1]

GUSTAVE COURBET

The story of Courbet's life is familiar to all who are interested in nineteenth-century French art. Born in Ornans, a small village near the Franco-Swiss border, Courbet came to Paris to become the champion of the new Realist movement of the mid-nineteenth century. A master of self-promotion, he managed to become one of the most talked-about artists of his time. Fiercely anti-establishment, he took on, in paintings like *A Burial at Ornans* (*Un enterrement à Ornans*; 1849–50, Musée d'Orsay, Paris), *The Bathers* (*Les Baigneuses*; 1853, Musée Fabre, Montpellier), and *The Return from the Conference* (*Le Retour de la conférence;* 1863, destroyed), such powerful French institutions as the Academy and the Church. After the dissolution of the Second Empire in September 1870, he recommended the removal of the Vendôme Column, hated symbol of Bonapartist imperialism (**FIG. 9.1**). Nine months later, as a member of the Paris Commune, he participated in the column's dismantlement. This last act of defiance cost him dearly and became the defining moment of the rest of his life and career.

AFTER THE FALL

For his participation in the Commune and the destruction of the Vendôme Column, Courbet was condemned to a fine and six months in prison. Having served his term, he returned to his native Franche-Comté region in the summer of 1872. As he was in dire need of money, he sold part of the contents of his Paris studio to the art dealer Paul Durand-Ruel.[2] He also embarked on the wholesale production of new works, mostly landscapes and still lifes. To maximize his productivity, he engaged the help of several landscape painters in the region, including François ("Jean-Jean") Cornu, Marcel Ordinaire, and Alexandre Rapin.[3] All three artists belonged to a colony of landscape artists who worked in and around Nans-sous-Sainte-Anne, a small village not far from Ornans.[4] Because their landscapes depicted sites that were similar to those painted by Courbet, they often superficially resembled the latter's works. Rapin's undated

FIG. **9.1** Bruno Braquehais, *Vendôme Column, Paris, with apparatus for toppling it*, 1871, photograph. Los Angeles, Getty Center. Courbet helped to dismantle the column in 1871, for which he was fined and sent to prison.

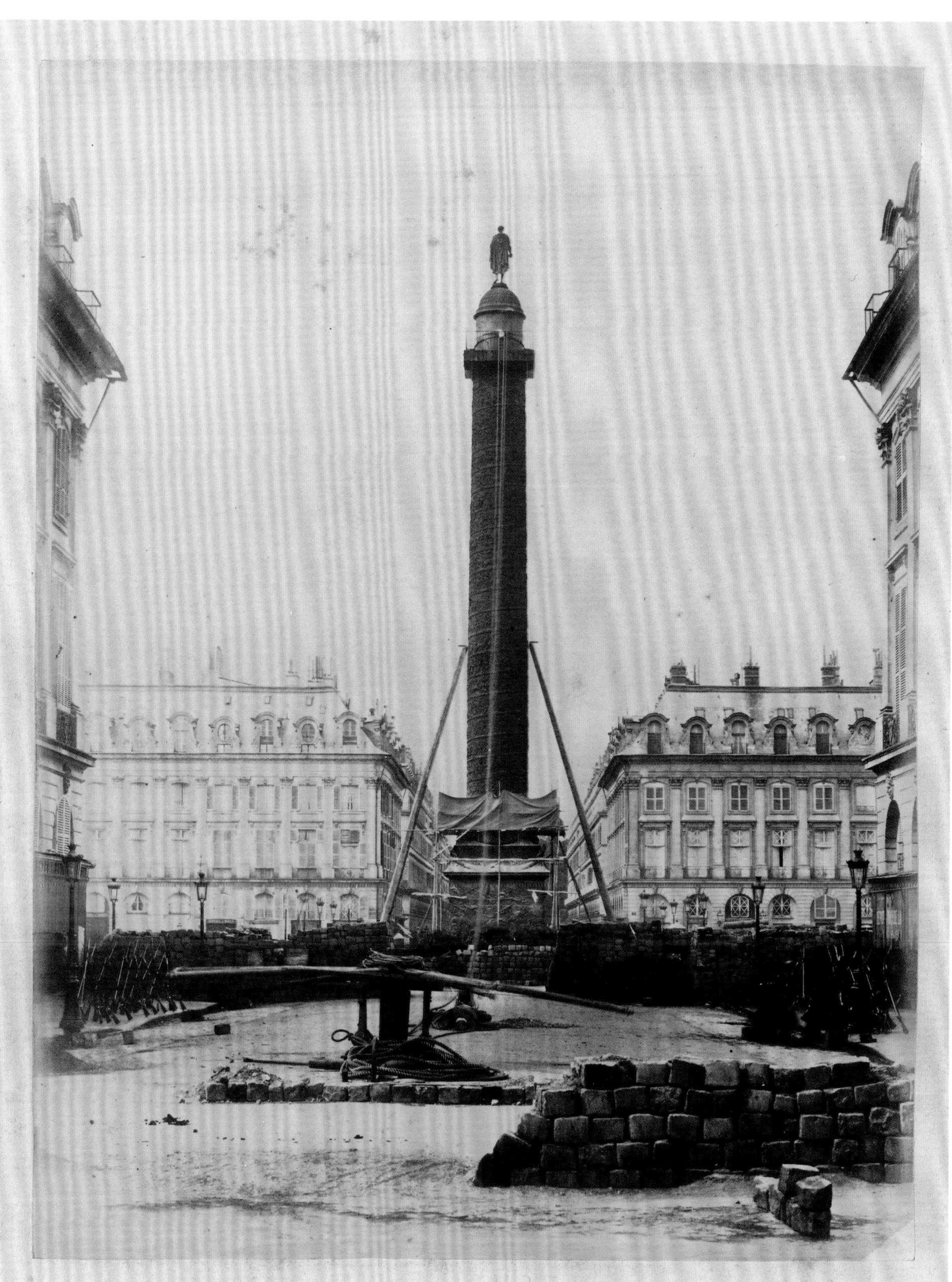

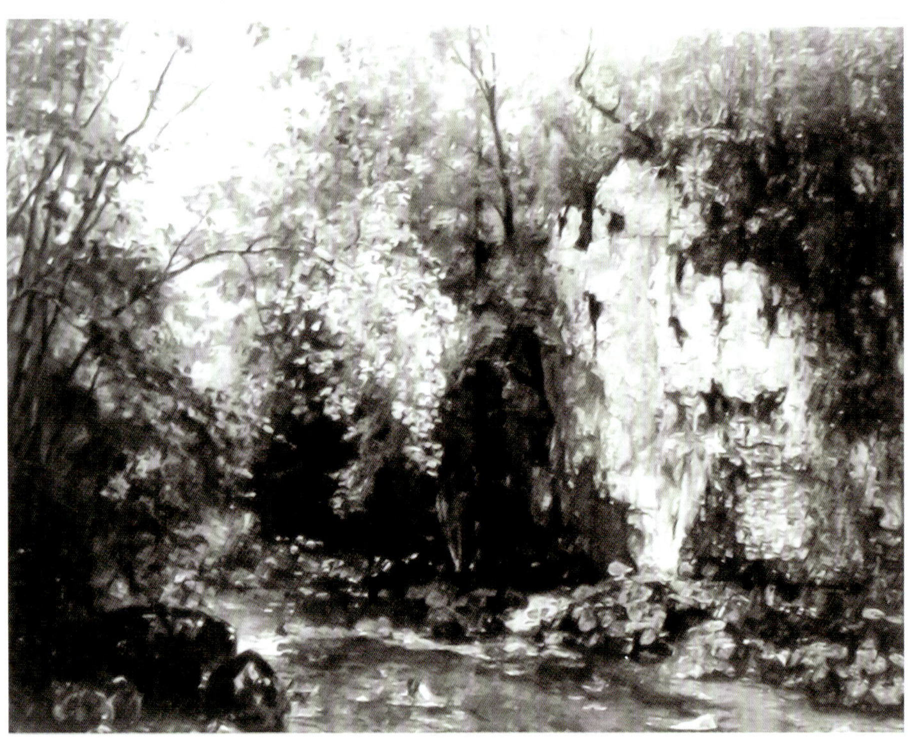

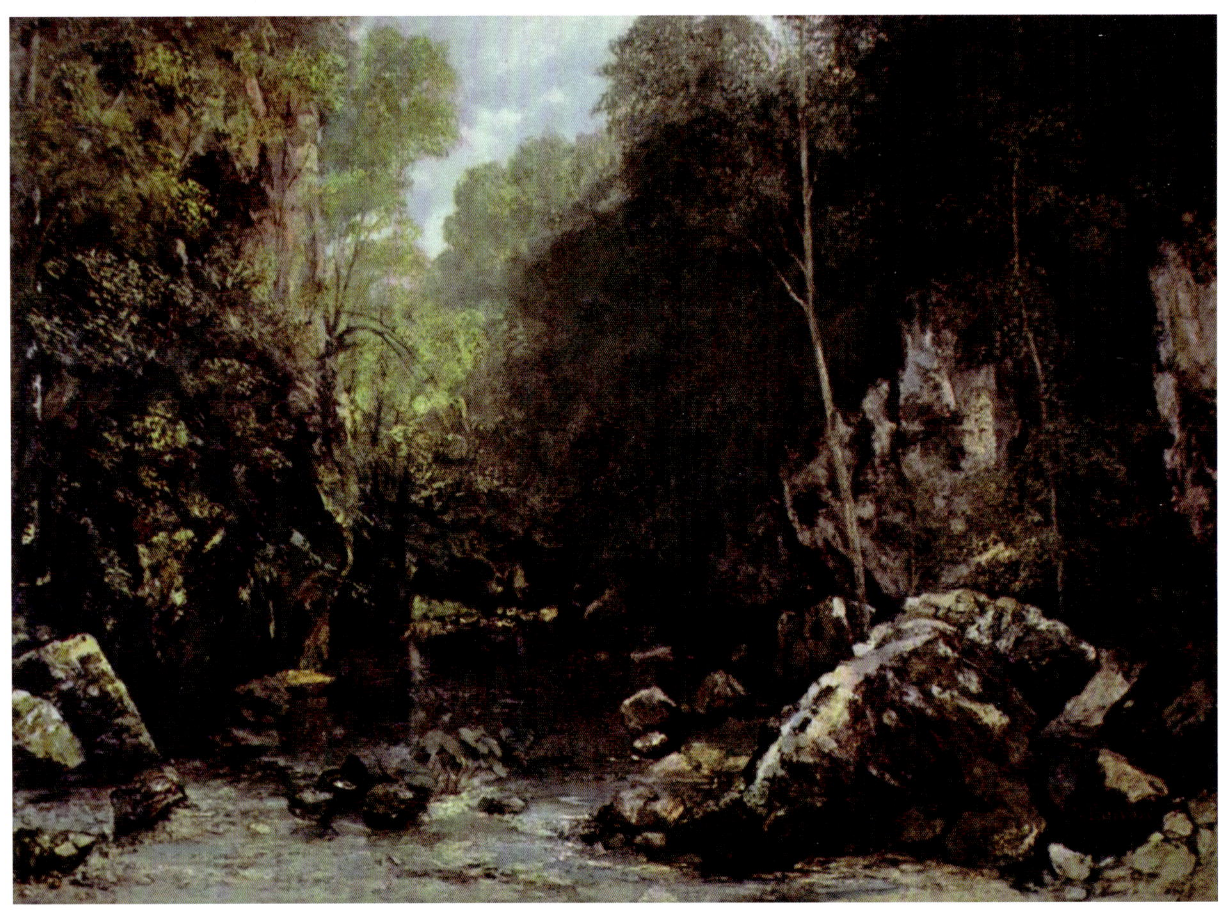

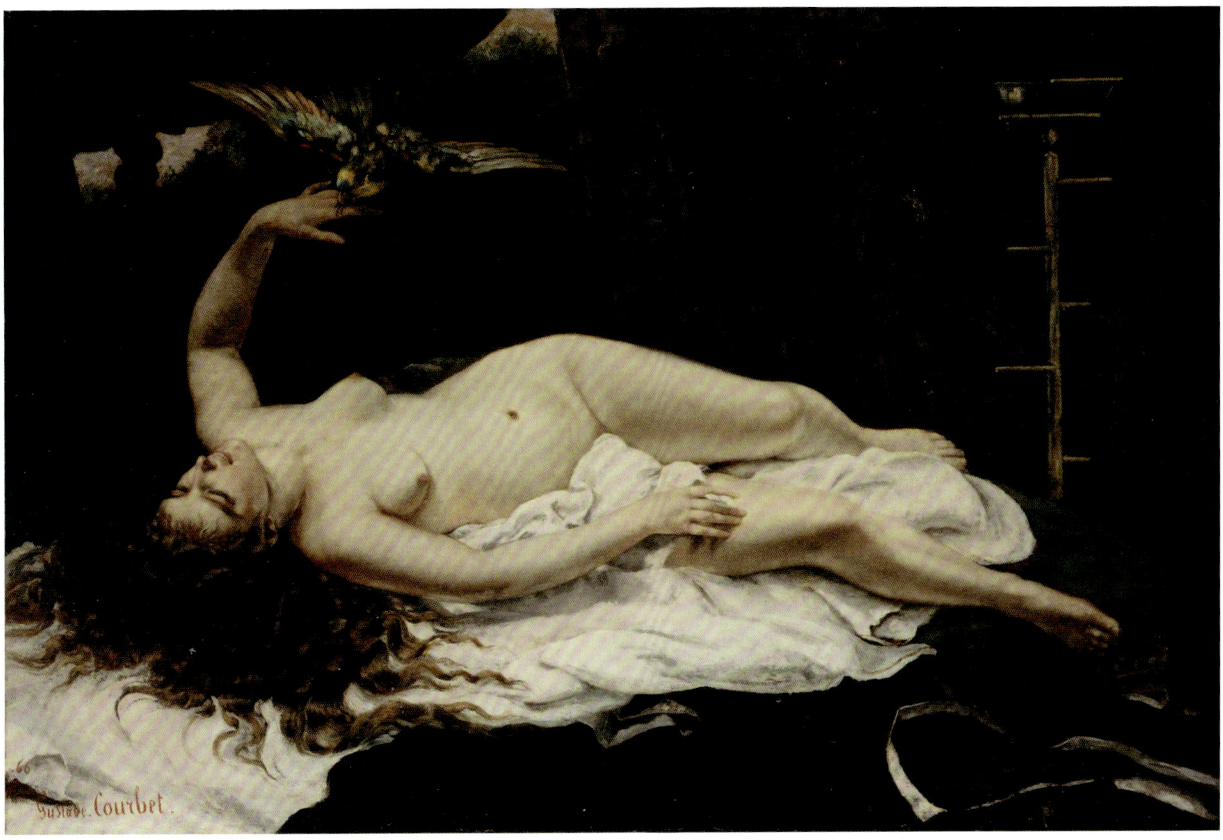

FIG. 9.2 Alexandre Rapin, *Puits-noir, Franche-Comté*, 1882?, oil on canvas, 55 ⅛ × 82 ¹¹⁄₁₆ in. (140 × 210 cm). Musée du Château, Montbéliard, 2016.13.1.

FIG. 9.3 Gustave Courbet, *Entrance of the Puits-noir Valley, Doubs, at Dusk*, 1865, oil on canvas, 37 × 53 ³⁄₁₆ in. (94 × 135 cm). Paris, Musée d'Orsay, RF 275.

FIG. 9.4 Gustave Courbet, *Woman with a Parrot*, 1866, oil on canvas, 51 × 77 in. (129.5 × 195.6 cm). Metropolitan Museum of Art, New York, H. O. Havemeyer Collection, Bequest of Mrs. H. O. Havemeyer, 1929, 29.100.57. Cherubino Pata copied this painting with Courbet's permission and later adopted Courbet's style and technique.

Puits-noir, Franche-Comté (**FIG. 9.2**), for example, calls to mind Courbet's paintings of the same motif (**FIG. 9.3**), though Rapin's is lighter and less broadly painted.

In addition to the three artists from his native region, Courbet was also joined by Cherubino Pata. Born in the Ticino region of Switzerland, Pata had studied at the École des Beaux-Arts in Lyon. From there he had traveled to Paris, where he first exhibited at the Salon of 1868. Some time in the late 1860s, he met Courbet, who granted him permission to copy the *Woman with a Parrot* (**FIG. 9.4**) in his atelier at the rue Hautefeuille. In due course, Pata became Courbet's factotum, involved in all aspects of the production and marketing of his master's work. When he first met Courbet, Pata painted pleasant landscapes in a belated Romantic mode (**FIG. 9.5**), but after 1870, he gradually adopted not only Courbet's subjects but also his style and technique (**FIG. 9.6**).

Little is known about the nature of the collaboration between Courbet and his "assistants." Sarah Faunce, author of one of

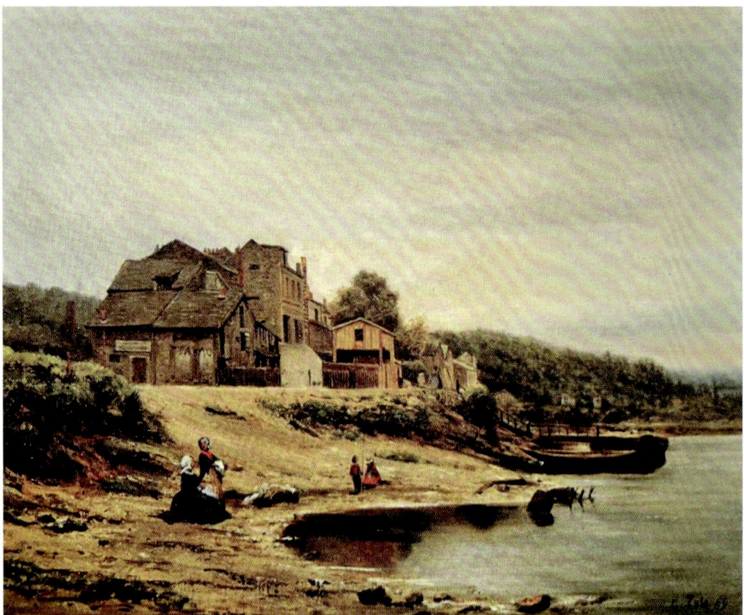

FIG. 9.5 Cherubino Pata, *Hamlet on a River Bank* (perhaps identical to *Bank of the Seine at Corbeil*, Salon of 1869). Current whereabouts unknown.

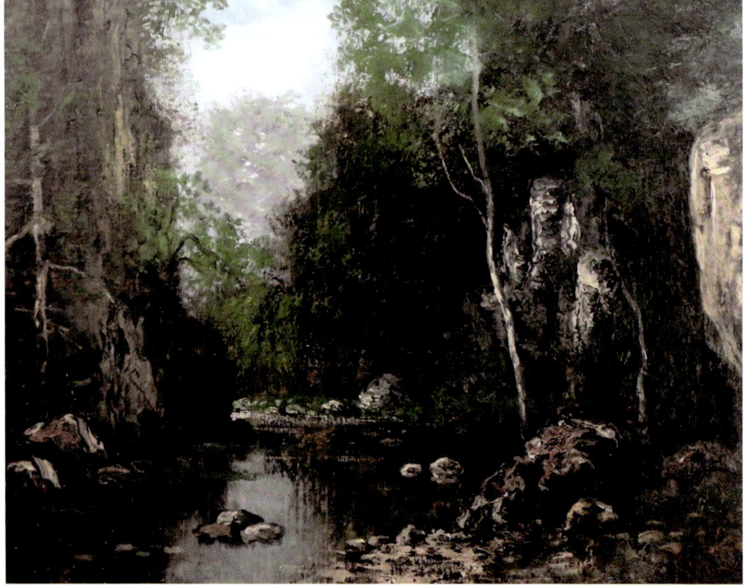

FIG. 9.6 Cherubino Pata, *The Puits-noir Valley*, ca. 1872?, oil on canvas, 19 ⅛ × 25 ⅜ in. (48.5 × 64.5 cm). Ornans, Musée Gustave Courbet.

the two forthcoming new catalogues raisonnés of Courbet's paintings (see below), is of the opinion that they did little more than stretch and coat canvases.[5] Her judgment is confirmed by a letter from Courbet to Pata (February 26, 1873), in which he asked his assistant to send him some small canvases with a "black undercoating."[6] That evidence notwithstanding, it is difficult to understand why Courbet needed the help of so many artists if stretching and coating canvases was all they did. Writing to his sisters in April 1873, Courbet consistently used the word "we," when talking about the production of his paintings. "We have no end of commissions"; or, "We have already delivered a score, we have as many still to deliver." In the same letter, he wrote that Cornu, Edouard, and Pata were "preparing" paintings, for which he paid them a percentage.[7] The question is what Courbet meant by "prepare." According to the artist's biographer Georges Riat, Courbet's assistants, especially Pata, did a great deal more than stretching and coating canvases. Riat even claims that Pata made finished landscapes, which were retouched and signed by Courbet.[8]

Several of the landscapes Courbet and his assistants produced in 1872 repeated motifs that the master had treated earlier. The catalogue raisonné of Courbet's work, published by Robert Fernier in 1977–78, reproduces a number of seascapes that bear Courbet's signature and the date 1872. Though the artist had visited the Normandy coast several times in the late 1860s and had painted numerous seascapes in Deauville and Trouville, he did not return there after 1870. That means that these paintings were entirely based on existing compositions. The same appears to have been true for many landscapes paintings of the Franche-Comté, dated in the same year, which also appear to be pure atelier productions.

COURBET IN SWITZERLAND

On May 30, 1873, the National Assembly of the French Third Republic passed a bill to re-erect the Vendôme Column. The bill contained a proviso that construction would start only after a civil tribunal had determined the financial responsibility of those—foremost Courbet—who had participated in its destruction. Pending the decision of the tribunal, the Minister of Finance ordered the sequestration of their assets. The seizure of

Courbet's property began on June 23. Having salvaged what he could, the artist left one month later for Switzerland, where he would live until his death in December 1877.

As he left France with little or no money, Courbet had to make a living in Switzerland by painting and selling new works. In Switzerland as in France, he appears to have surrounded himself with assistants, who helped him in a variety of ways. Among them were Marcel Ordinaire, who had followed him to Switzerland, as well as the French painter Ernest-Paul Brigot and the Polish André Slomszynski or "Slom."[9] Pata, his faithful aid, traveled back and forth between France and Switzerland, to look after his affairs.

In Switzerland, Courbet found dealers in Paul Pia, an exiled French engineer, who had opened a gallery in Geneva; as well as in Gustave Pétrequin-Dard, a painter and part-time art dealer in Lausanne. The Swiss market was limited, however, and Courbet had to look for buyers elsewhere—especially in France and England. International sales presented their own problems, as it was difficult to send paintings across the French border for fear of seizure. To smuggle them into the country, Courbet and his assistants, most notably Pata, invented ingenious systems. The painter Ernest Biéler recalled how Courbet hid his signature underneath a piece of cigarette paper, which he subsequently covered with paint.[10] According to Jean-Jacques Fernier, the artist would also ship unsigned works to France, asking Pata to add his initials or a full signature later. Alternatively, he would provide Pata with signed certificates that the latter could glue on the back of the paintings once they had arrived in France.[11]

Such practices obviously led to confusion and encouraged fraud. If Courbet himself allowed others to sign his paintings, what prevented artists or dealers from putting his name to works they themselves had painted or owned? As early as 1873, his friend Castagnary sent a letter to Courbet warning him that many *faux Courbet* were being sold in Paris.[12] He blamed Courbet's assistants for their dishonesty, but it is more likely that crooked dealers affixed the master's name to canvases by his followers. Among them may have been Alexandre Bernheim, a dealer on the rue Lafitte in Paris, whom Courbet accused of filling Paris with forgeries of his paintings.[13] Several examples of canvases bearing phony Courbet signatures have been discovered in recent years. A *Jura Landscape* in the Art Institute of Chicago (**FIG. 9.7**), for example, was found, in the course of restoration, to have an overpainted signature of Marcel Ordinaire in the lower right corner, and, in the lower left, the signature of Courbet and a date, "..67."

While Courbet's followers and unscrupulous dealers were merrily adding works to the artist's oeuvre, professional forgers were also busy producing Courbet landscapes and still lifes, for which there appears to have been an insatiable market. For despite Courbet's political extremism or, perhaps, because of it, his already-high visibility had increased and led to a steady demand for his works. As early as June 16, 1874, an article in *La République française* claimed that a "factory" of Courbet

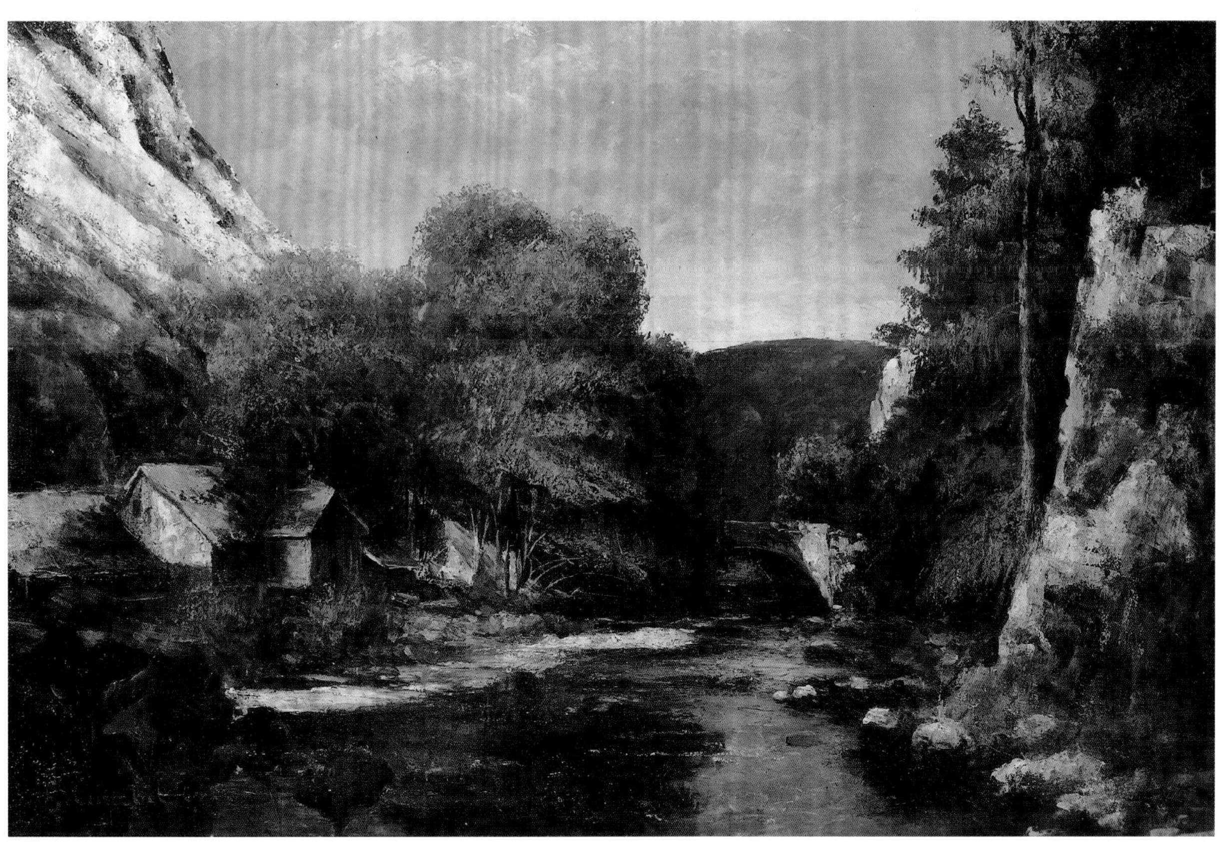

FIG. 9.7 Marcel Ordinaire, *Jura Landscape*, n.d., oil on canvas, 21 × 40 ¾ in. (53.5 × 81 cm). Art Institute of Chicago, Bequest of Joseph Winterbotham, 1954.306. Signed lower left "G. Courbet ..67." Restoration revealed signature lower right, "Marcel Ordinaire."

counterfeits had been established in Geneva. Courbet's dealer
Paul Pia immediately sent a response, countersigned by Courbet,
asserting that his shop in Geneva had nothing to do with those
phony Courbets. They could do little, however, to stop the
production of fakes. The forgery of Courbet's work continued
unabated even after his death. An article in *Le Temps* of August
26, 1890, entitled "Le Commerce des faux Courbet," describes
the discovery by Courbet's sister Juliette of a brisk trade in
Courbet fakes in Brussels.[14] Apparently, these forgeries were
produced in and around Paris, where a "cartel" of artists made
a specialty of producing various types of Courbet landscapes.
One of them specialized in "light greens," another in *sous–bois* and
"mossy rocks," and a third in wooded landscapes with deer
and other animals.[15] The article also implicates a former
"student and friend" of Courbet (perhaps Pata?), who is accused
of imitating the work of his master so well that one of his *falaises*
was accepted by the jury of the French art show at the
International Exposition of 1889, while an authentic work by
Courbet was refused.[16]

It is clear from the above that all who study Courbet's late
works, especially his landscapes, must be aware of the attribution
problems they present. Such works may be:

1. Works by his own hand with an authentic signature ("G.
   Courbet" or just his initials, "G. C.").[17]
2. Works by his own hand with a forged signature (see above).
3. Works painted by his assistants, retouched by Courbet and
   bearing his authentic signature.
4. Works begun by Courbet and finished by his assistants,
   bearing his authentic signature. Jean-Jacques Fernier
   believes that such works date from the very end of
   Courbet's career, when, worn down by his legal problems
   and suffering from various alcohol-induced ailments,
   Courbet was unable to deliver works and had his assistants
   finish them.[18]

5. Works painted by his assistants, with a forged signature. Such signatures may have been applied by Courbet's followers themselves. More often than not, however, they seem to have been added by dealers who removed the original signature and added Courbet's.

6. Forgeries by artists other than his assistants, painted anytime between the 1870s and the present.

DOCUMENTATION AND BENCHMARKING

Few Courbet paintings of the 1870s have a documented history. The artist rarely took part in exhibitions after his works were rejected from the Salon of 1872 and the International Exposition in Vienna in 1873. To the ones in which he did participate, such as the exhibition of the Austrian Art Union (Österreichischer Kunst-Verein) in 1873, he mostly sent earlier works. Only a handful of his late paintings are known to have been shown by the artist in public between 1873 and his death in 1877.[19] Courbet's letters, which before 1872 had contained much information about works in progress, rarely touched on the subject after that date. The artist's voluminous correspondence of the 1870s deals nearly exclusively with his legal problems. Last but not least, few works of the 1870s have a reliable provenance that allows us to trace their ownership history back to the artist. All this means that there are not many works of the 1870s that can be attributed to Courbet with certainty and can serve as a touchstone against which to measure others.

It is true that, upon Courbet's death, an inventory was made of the works in his studio by Dr. Blondon, a friend of the artist's family.[20] This list is especially helpful to identify the portraits and figure paintings Courbet painted during his stay in Switzerland. Among them are, for example, the portrait of Courbet's father in the Petit Palais in Paris, and the *Vigneronne de Montreux* in the Musée Cantonale in Lausanne, both painted in 1874. It is less useful for the landscape paintings, as the titles are frequently vague and nondescript, and many entries lack dimensions. Moreover, it is not certain that all the paintings included in

Blondon's list were completely authentic. Nonetheless, this list,
in combination with other data, allows us to identify some works
with a good deal of certainty, among them the large sketch of the
Dents du Midi (1877), now in the Cleveland Museum of Art,
and the *Château de Chillon* (1874) in the Musée Gustave
Courbet in Ornans.

In studying the late works that can be attributed to the artist
with certainty, it is clear that, until ill health prevented him from
painting altogether, Courbet did not lose any of his faculties,
despite his severe alcoholism. This becomes clear when one looks
at the beautiful *Sunset, Vevey, Switzerland* (*Coucher de soleil, Vevey,
Suisse*; **FIG. 9.8**) in the Cincinnati Art Museum, a painting that is
on a par with the best seascapes Courbet produced in Trouville, on

FIG. 9.8 Gustave Courbet, *Sunset, Vevey,
Switzerland*, 1874, oil on canvas, 25 ¾ × 32 in.
(65.4 × 81.3 cm). Cincinnati Art Museum, Gift of
George Hoadly, 1887.5.

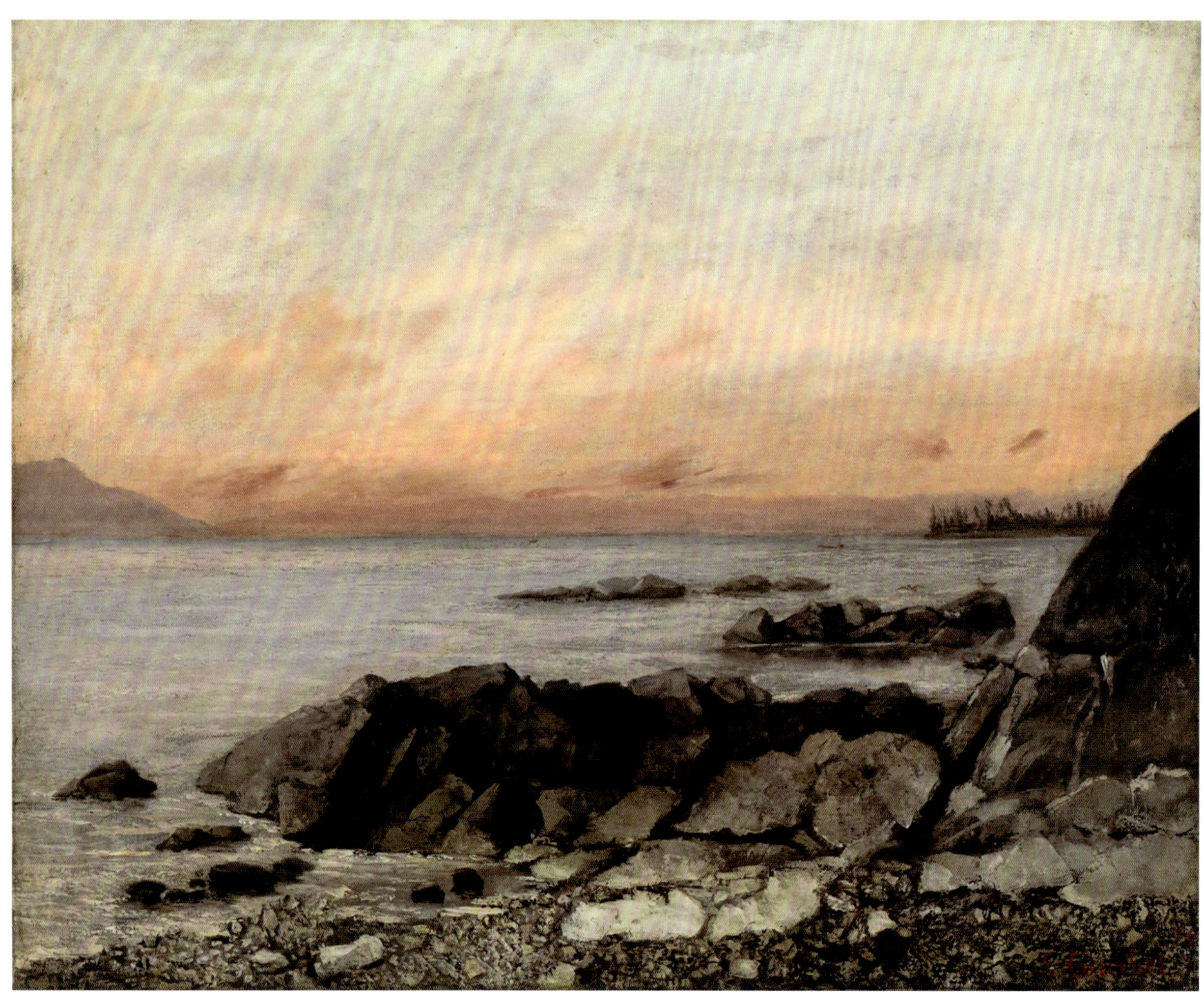

the Normandy Coast, in the late 1860s. *Sunset, Vevey* was bought
from the artist by the American journalist Moncure Conway,
acting on behalf of Judge George Hoadley, the future governor of
Ohio, who had become interested in Courbet for his politics.
When Conway visited Courbet in the winter of 1874, the
journalist expressed a preference for Courbet's figure paintings,
finding the artist's mountain scenes "powerful but with somber
tone." To this, the artist responded tellingly: "I cannot insert a
figure in the presence of these grand mountains. It would belittle
them. And, indeed, since I left Ornans I have no heart to paint
human figures."[21]

PROVENANCE

While provenances are helpful in guaranteeing the authenticity
of works of art, they can also be problematic and must always
be judged at face value and on a case-by-case basis. In Courbet's
case, this is especially important. As he was the victim of the
deceit of some of his closest relatives and companions, it is often
not sufficient to retrace the provenance of a work to one of
the artist's family members or friends—it must go back to the
artist himself.

Case in point: some twenty years ago, an exhibition held in
the museums of Baden-Baden and Zürich presented a newly
discovered cache of drawings and oil sketches by Courbet.
Organized by Klaus Herding and Katharina Schmidt, *Les Voyages
secrets de Monsieur Courbet* featured works whose provenance
went back to Courbet's sister Zoé.[22] Moreover, all drawings and
sketches bore the following stamp: "*Hoirie Courbet,*" or "Succession
Courbet." While the stamp and the provenance were adduced as
proofs of the attribution of these drawings and sketches to
Courbet, in fact they were far from conclusive. The stamp is
not found on any other work by Courbet, and the word "hoirie,"
is atypical of atelier stamps of the nineteenth century. The
provenance also raised questions because Zoé is known to have
had a very hostile relationship with her brother, especially during
his final years. Courbet's letters of the 1870s refer repeatedly to

the attempts of Zoé and her husband, Eugène Reverdy, to swindle him in every way possible. As a consequence, Courbet excluded her from his will, leaving all his assets to his sister Juliette.

Today, it is generally accepted that the drawings and sketches shown in the Baden-Baden and Zürich exhibitions are not by Courbet. Instead, they may have been the work of Reverdy, a minor and completely forgotten painter.[23] It is difficult to determine who was responsible for putting the *Hoirie Courbet* stamp on these works and for marketing them as Courbets, and it is not relevant here. What *is* important is that the case underscores the need for the provenance to be traced back to Courbet himself.

Separating the true Courbets from the false is the self-imposed task of the authors who have embarked on the artist's catalogues raisonnés. One such catalogue was prepared by the late Robert Fernier, who undertook his task under the auspices of the Fondation Wildenstein in Paris. Fernier, a painter who cooperated with the art historian Gaston Delestre until the latter's death in 1969, did a yeoman's job of documenting and researching Courbet paintings across Europe, Canada, and the eastern seaboard of the United States. His two-volume catalogue raisonné, published in 1977–78, is still an indispensable reference work for those who study Courbet's paintings, but it is no longer considered authoritative.

Fernier's son Jean-Jacques, architect, curator of the Musée Courbet at Ornans, and president of the Amis de Gustave Courbet, is currently working on a revised edition of his father's catalogue. His plan is to abandon the chronological classification and to replace it with a thematic ordering.[24] This strategy allows the reader to compare Courbet's numerous versions of different themes, such as his views of the Puits-noir, the Norman coast, waves, the source of the Loue river, etc.

Over the past twenty years, Jean-Jacques Fernier has done more than anyone to confront the issue of Courbet and his collaborators. In 1988, he organized an exhibition in Ornans entitled *Cherubino Pata, ou le vrai-faux Courbet.* The book published in conjunction with this exhibition includes an inventory of Pata's works. The majority of the paintings inventoried bear Courbet's signature or initials. Naturally, not everyone agrees with Fernier about his rigorous reattribution of "Courbets" to Pata. Nonetheless, he has focused attention on the complex attribution problems posed by Courbet's late work, and he has raised the possibility that many paintings currently attributed to the master were actually the work of his students, if not of deliberate forgers.

Meanwhile, in New York, Sarah Faunce, curator emeritus of the Brooklyn Museum, has been working since 1998 on an entirely new catalogue raisonné of Courbet's paintings. Faunce has the advantage that much of her groundwork has already been done. She thus can spend more time documenting Courbet's paintings, a task that is essential for the proper attribution of the artist's works. It is hoped that her work will result in the expansion of the number of late works that can be irrefutably attributed to Courbet so that a clearer picture will emerge of the characteristics of the artist's late style.

CONCLUSION

Documentation is as important for the authentication of Courbet's paintings as it is for any other artist. Provenance, exhibition history, the mention of works in the artist's correspondence, their presence on inventories of the contents of the artist's studio— these are all forms of documentation that, if not a guarantee, at least affirm the attribution of a work to the artist. The formation of a clearer picture of Courbet's late style is dependent on the establishment of a critical mass of authentic works that will help discerning critics attribute undocumented works to the artist on the basis of well-founded visual comparisons.

Originally published in the *IFAR Journal 7*, no. 1 (2004), this text is reproduced by the Arthur Ross Gallery with the permission of the International Foundation for Art Research (IFAR) and may not be published or printed elsewhere without the express permission of IFAR. The text has been slightly edited to conform to the style of the present volume. No changes have been made to the content; it is noteworthy that some of the information regarding the Courbet catalogue raisonné projects is now outdated.

This article was written during time spent as a fellow at the Netherlands Institute for Advanced Study in Wassenaar. I am extremely grateful to NIAS for five months of uninterrupted time to write and reflect. My thanks go as well to Seton Hall University for allowing me a one-semester leave of absence.

1. In writing this article, I have profited greatly from the following works: Robert Fernier, *La Vie et oeuvre de Gustave Courbet: Catalogue raisonné*, 2 vols. (Lausanne: Bibliothèque des arts; Fondation Wildenstein, 1977–78); Pierre Chessex and Paul-André Jaccard, *Courbet et la Suisse*, exh. cat. (La Tour-de-Peilz: P. Chessex, 1982); Klaus Herding, "Zu Courbets Spätwerk," *Pantheon* 44 (1986): 75–86; Jean-Jacques Fernier, *Cherubino Pata (1827–1899), ou le vrai-faux Courbet*, exh. cat. (Ornans: Musée Courbet, 1988); Annie Agache, "Antonin Fanart et son temps: Étude d'un paysagiste comtois et contribution à la vie sociale en Franche-Comté au XIXème siècle" (PhD diss., Université NR, Besançon, 1990); Petra ten-Doesschate Chu, ed., *Letters of Gustave Courbet* (Chicago: University of Chicago Press, 1996); Jean-Jacques Fernier, "The Natures of Courbet," in *Courbet: The Late Paintings*, exh. cat. (New York: Salander-O'Reilly Galleries, 1998); and Claudette Mainzer, "Les Suiveurs de Courbet," in *Gustave Courbet et la Franche-Comté*, exh. cat. (Besançon: Musée des Beaux-Arts, 2000).

2. A separate article could be devoted to the fate of the contents of Courbet's Paris studio after the artist's arrest and imprisonment. It is an extremely complex story that also has a bearing on the authentication of his works, most notably the ones of the 1860s.

3. On August 14, Courbet informed his friend Jules Castagnary that Rapin, Cornu, Pata, and some unnamed Swiss artists had joined him in the Franche-Comté. See Chu, *Letters of Gustave Courbet*, 464.

4. On the artists' colony of Nanssous-Sainte-Anne, see Agache, "Antonin Fanart et son temps," 279–81.

5. Telephone conversation, January 2004.

6. Chu, *Letters of Gustave Courbet*, 489.

7. Chu, *Letters of Gustave Courbet*, 495.

8. Georges Riat, *Gustave Courbet, peintre* (Paris: H. Floury, 1906), 344.

9. Fernier, *Cherubino Pata*, 88, mentions several other artists, but it is difficult to assess the role of assistants during Courbet's Swiss period as there is little documentary information. Perhaps the most important document alluding to collaboration is a letter by Brigot, written on March 4, 1874, in which he wrote to Courbet, "I have heard from Castagnary that you have many orders and not enough time. If you would like a strong helping hand, I'd be at your disposal. I don't need to tell you that together we would get a lot of work done. I have about four or five months ahead of me." Fernier, *Cherubino Pata*, 90. Translation by the author. Another important document is an announcement on p. 24 of *Les Beaux-Arts en Suisse en 1874*, published in Bern in 1875, that reads: "Courbet and his pupil Patta [*sic*] have opened their atelier in La Tour-de-Peilz near Vevey, after having lived for some time in the Valais region." Cited in Pierre Chessex, "Courbet en Eldorado: Les années d'exil en Suisse, 1873–1877," *Ligeia: Dossiers sur l'art* 41–44 (October 2002–June 2003): 84. Translation by the author.

10. Cited in Fernier, *Cherubino Pata*, 40.

11. See Fernier, *Cherubino Pata*, 86–87; and Fernier, "Natures of Courbet," 22.

12. Riat, *Gustave Courbet, peintre*, 344.

13. In a letter to Jules Castagnary of March 26, 1874. Chu, *Letters of Gustave Courbet*, 525.

14. For a full text of the article, see Fernier, *La Vie et oeuvre*, 2:340–41.

15. Fernier, *La Vie et oeuvre*, 2:340.

16. I have been unable to verify this assertion.

17. For samples of Courbet's signatures, see Fernier, *La Vie et oeuvre*, 2:333–37. Only in a few instances did Courbet use his full signature, "Gustave Courbet."

18. Fernier, "Natures of Courbet," 22.

19. For an in-depth discussion of Courbet's exhibition activity in Switzerland, see Chessex and Jaccard, *Courbet et la Suisse*, 47–66.

20. The list, which also includes the paintings that were in the shop of Paul Pia, was copied and annotated by Charles Léger in *Courbet et son temps* (Paris: Éditions universelles, 1948), 165–69. Léger added a list of his own (169–73), which, done seventy years after Courbet's death, may be less reliable. Blondon's original list and other notes may be found in the Bibliothèque de Besançon.

21. Moncure D. Conway, *The Autobiography of Moncure D. Conway* (Boston: Houghton, Mifflin, 1904), 1:251.

22. Klaus Herding und Katharina Schmidt, *Les Voyages secrets de Monsieur Courbet: Unbekannte*

Reiseskizzen aus Baden, Spa und Biarritz, exh. cat. (Baden-Baden: Staatliche Kunsthalle, 1984).

23. On the arguments for Reverdy's authorship, see my review of the exhibition in *Master Drawings* 22, no. 4 (1984): 455–61.

24. See Marie-Christine Maufus, "Le Wildenstein Institute et le nouveau catalogue de l'oeuvre de Gustave Courbet," *Ligeia: Dossiers sur l'art* 41–44 (October 2002–June 2003): 176–77.

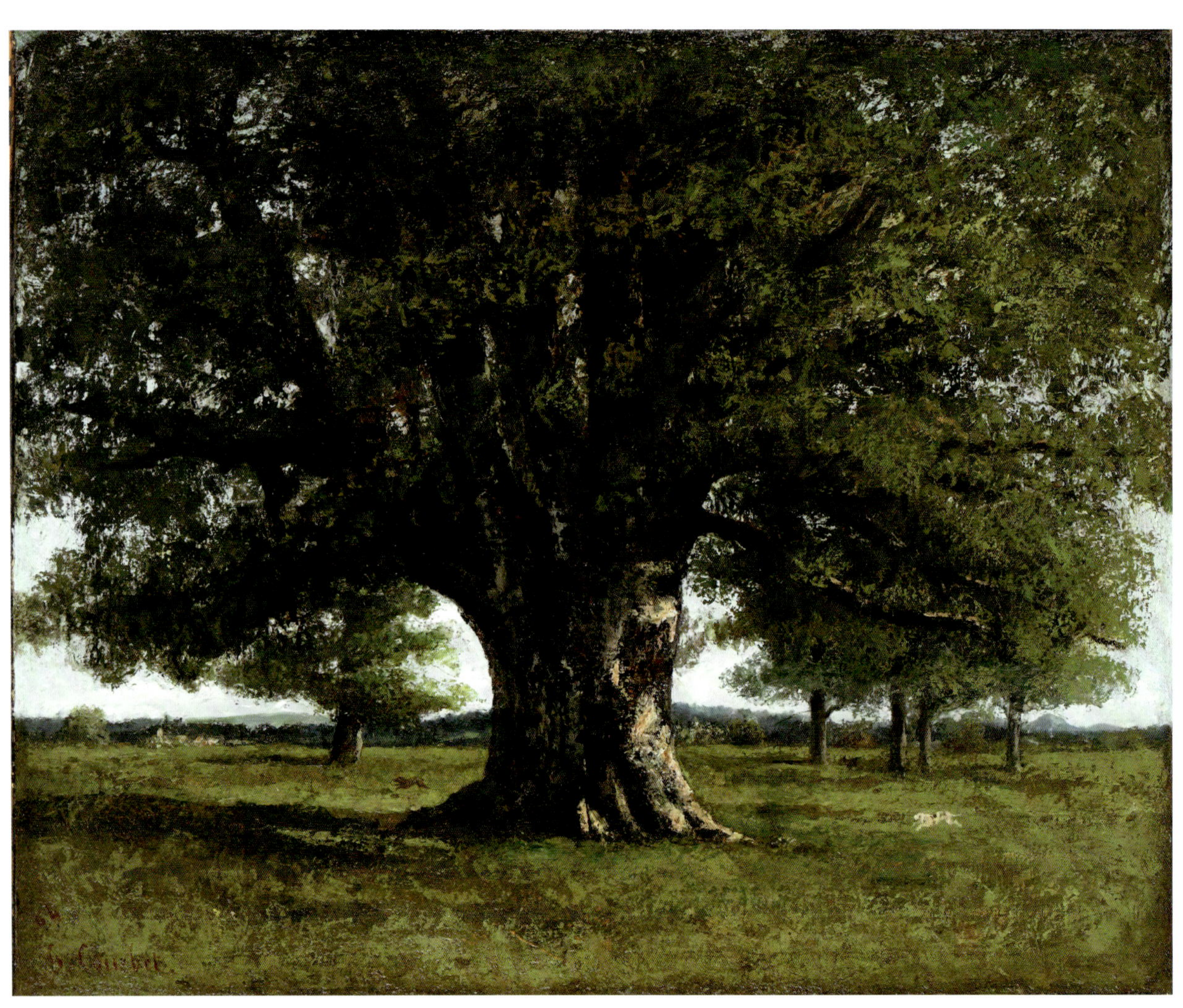

UNSETTLED GROUND:
The Development of Courbet Landscape Studies

JALEN CHANG

In the more than one hundred years since the last documented appearance of the University of Pennsylvania's *The Source of the Lison* (*La Source du Lison*; see fig. 1.1), scholarly estimations of Courbet's landscapes have reached peaks and valleys alike. Consider, for example, an apex—the art historian Émile Michel's appraisal in 1906: "There is no need here to speak of [Courbet] the figure painter, of his exorbitant pretensions, of that doctrine of realism of which he proclaimed himself the apostle yet was unable to define, of his complete absence of taste and of sense of proportion. . . . Quite fortunately, we need here only to consider the landscape painter."[1] Michel's Manichean view of Courbet's oeuvre is, in fact, quite complex in its apparent simplicity. As Linda Nochlin has shown, it was preconditioned by a trend of "rehabilitation" and "depoliticization" initiated by late nineteenth-century critics and Republican art administrators.[2] When Michel elevated later landscapes such as *The Source of the Lison* and denigrated the now-canonical 1840s and 1850s figure paintings like *A Burial at Ornans* (*Un enterrement à Ornans*; 1849–50, Musée d'Orsay, Paris), he contributed to a romantic discursive construction of Courbet as an heir to the French landscape tradition.[3] This tasteful, defanged *paysagiste* Courbet superseded the Courbets that have become familiar again to us today: the avant-garde painter of French social structure, the ambivalent stager of rural-urban conflict, the Communard.[4]

Courbet's legacy as an inaugural modernist derives in part from a similarly dichotomous position on his oeuvre, one

FIG. 10.1 Gustave Courbet, *The Oak of Flagey*, also known as *The Vercingetorix Oak, Caesar's Camp near Alesia*, 1864, oil on canvas, 35 × 43 ⅞ in. (89 × 111.5 cm). Musée Gustave Courbet, inv. 2013.1.1.

promulgated by 1970s and 1980s social art history that gave pride of place to his figural work.[5] Thrown into relief against the artist's invigorating modernism was the profile of a "late Courbet"—the churner-out of ultimately meaningless landscapes that trafficked in repetition, performative materiality, and pandering to bourgeois patrons who sought an easily consumable fiction of Nature.[6] Anne Wagner's 1981 article "Courbet's Landscapes and Their Markets" is the most empirically substantiated case for this position,[7] yet the stance is perhaps most succinctly expressed by T. J. Clark's backhanded compliment to the landscapes from 1973: "Courbet's landscape style was in fact an integral part of his Realism. Its failure, for it seems to me the weakest part of Courbet's art, is almost necessary to the figure paintings' success."[8] Clark and Michel's opposing, rather vociferous takes on Courbet's oeuvre illustrate a long-running inclination to divide and subsequently hierarchize the artist's output. Furthermore, their contrast points toward what would become a prominent strand of Courbet scholarship from the 1970s onward—the reconciliatory attempt to understand the rich complexities of Courbet's early modernism as equally bound up in landscapes such as *The Source of the Lison* as in the monumental figure paintings.[9]

While Clark's account of Courbet summoned the landscapes for their subsequent dismissal, Klaus Herding gave them unprecedented attention in a pathbreaking article two years later, subsequently translated as "Equality and Authority in Courbet's Landscape Painting."[10] Contra Clark, Herding saw Courbet's landscapes as "anarchist" tableaux that effectively transubstantiated the monumental figure paintings' politics and formal innovations.[11] In this view, Courbet's landscape ethic eschewed hierarchy and claims to human authority, rebuking academic conventions of centralized narrative and naturalistic color application through his avant-garde technique. Furthermore, Herding posited that Courbet's favored subjects in the Jura and Doubs implicitly valorized a regionalist independence in defiance of the centripetal forces of Second Empire modernization. Thus, pictures such as

The Source of the Lison are seen less as market-driven ploys and more as coded political statements in their own right, landscapes that model in their very focus and facture a naturalized, territorialist egalitarianism.[12]

The specifics of place in Courbet's landscapes were further examined by Nochlin and Petra ten-Doesschate Chu. Adjacent to Herding, Nochlin revealed a pointed anti-imperial charge in *The Oak of Flagey* (*Le Chêne de Flagey*; **FIG. 10.1**), which claimed for the Franche-Comté the historic site of the Gallic last stand against Caesar. Yet Nochlin also remained alert to the gamut of registers on which Courbet's favored territories signified, elucidating the gendered visual structures of his Doubs Source paintings and his Normandy "landscapes of the sea" (*paysages de mer*; see fig. 5.6).[13] In a series of foundational publications, Chu further contextualized the painter's engagement with the Franche-Comté, claiming that Courbet's very landscape vision was conditioned by a lifetime of confronting his changing natural environs. Courbet's landscapes captured the intertwined effects on nature of slow-moving geological processes and accelerating human industry—dual concerns shared by a cadre of learned, economically prosperous Doubs natives for whom some of the Franche-Comté works may have been intended.[14] In a similar vein, Chu also argued for the regional particularities of Courbet's landscape recipients beyond Wagner's burned-out urban businessman. Preternaturally attentive to a diverse clientele and a modernizing art market, Courbet produced pictures that satisfied different desires for tourists versus sportsmen, Britons versus Germans, and Parisians versus fellow Comtois.[15]

A historiography of Courbet's landscapes must also mention the strand of scholarship on the corporeal, phenomenological cast of his painting, most notably the work of Michael Fried. Along this line of thinking, the landscapes exceed specific materializations of geological vision, territorial claims of identity, or rhetorics of gendered bodies. In the last analysis, they operate on the alleged core mechanism of Courbet's oeuvre—the never-quite-attainable goal of inserting oneself (as artist or beholder) into the representational space of the artwork. While Fried displays some familiar divisionist tendencies, stating clearly that Courbet "wasn't essentially a landscapist but a figure painter," his system nonetheless affords to a picture such as *The Source of the Lison* a similarly vaunted goal as to a canonical work such as *The Painter's Studio* (*L'Atelier du peintre*; see fig. 5.4): the exploration of the durational push and pull exerted by a work of art with an enigmatic center.[16]

The most recent scholarship on Courbet's landscapes centers on the very brushstrokes that originally drew charges of meaninglessness from Clark and Wagner, and it follows Chu, Fried, Nochlin, and Herding in giving Courbet's physical mark making its full intellectual due. Anthea Callen has historicized Courbet's palette-knife technique, from its associations with provincial, *déclassé* labor unbefitting of a traditionally successful French painter, to its masculinist charge in relation to feminine-coded nature, through its influence on post-Impressionist landscapists such as Cézanne.[17] Paul Galvez has taken this line of analysis even farther in his monograph on Courbet's 1860s canvases, seeing in the artist's painstakingly materialist landscape technique a thoroughly modernist investigation into the "problem of the origin," or the unstable relationship between the worlds of reality and representation that inhere in and on a painted surface.[18]

The Source of the Lison, therefore, reemerges into view during a rich moment for Courbet landscape scholarship.[19] The state of the field does not reduce the work to an unremarkable copy, a cynical tourist fiction, or a descent from Courbet's avant-garde heights. Rather, the past fifty years of writing on Courbet's landscapes have primed the work for rigorous, multifaceted examination—a well-equipped journey for meaning into the seemingly endless cavern of the source.

1. Émile Michel, *Les Maîtres du paysage* (Paris: Hachette, 1906), 1:484–85.

2. Linda Nochlin, "The De-Politicization of Gustave Courbet: Transformation and Rehabilitation under the Third Republic," *October* 22 (Fall 1982): 64–78; reprinted in Linda Nochlin, *Courbet* (New York: Thames & Hudson, 2007), 116–27.

3. Of course, the history of Courbet's landscapes and that of his figure paintings cannot be so easily separated. For example, on the centrality of landscape in *The Painter's Studio*, see Mary Morton, "To Create a Living Art: Rethinking Courbet's Landscape Painting," in *Courbet and the Modern Landscape*, ed. Mary Morton and Charlotte Eyerman, exh. cat. (Los Angeles: Getty Publications, 2006), 1–19; and Petra ten-Doesschate Chu, "Showing Making in Courbet's *The Painter's Studio*," in *Hiding Making—Showing Creation: The Studio from Turner to Tacita Dean*, ed. Rachel Esner, Sandra Kisters, and Ann-Sophie Lehmann (Amsterdam: Amsterdam University Press, 2013), 62–72.

4. It is not difficult to imagine Thomas W. Evans—noted friend (and dentist) to the most exclusive circles of Second Empire France—being influenced by these critical currents of depoliticization when purchasing for his collection the Courbet landscape now at the University of Pennsylvania.

5. Meyer Schapiro's 1941 article "Courbet and Popular Imagery" is often credited with launching the scholarly bias toward Courbet's figure paintings. Meyer Schapiro, "Courbet and Popular Imagery: An Essay on Realism and Naïveté," *Journal of the Warburg and Courtauld Institutes* 4, no. 3–4 (April 1941–July 1942): 164–91.

6. This is not to say that Courbet only painted landscapes later in his career. However, the vast majority of Courbet landscape scholarship focuses on the 1860s onward, the period of greatest output in the genre. See Morton, "To Create a Living Art," 17n14.

7. Anne Wagner, "Courbet's Landscapes and Their Markets," *Art History* 4, no. 4 (1981): 410–31.

8. T. J. Clark, *Image of the People: Gustave Courbet and the 1848 Revolution*, 3rd edition (Berkeley: University of California Press, 1999), 132.

9. In his recent book *Courbet's Landscapes: The Origins of Modern Painting* (New Haven, CT: Yale University Press, 2022), Paul Galvez includes in his introduction an excellent, thorough primer on the major conceptual loci of Courbet landscape studies since the 1940s.

10. Klaus Herding, "Egalität und Autorität in Courbets Landschafts-malerei," *Städel-Jahrbuch* 5 (1975): 159–99, translated and reprinted as "Equality and Authority in Courbet's Landscape Painting," in *Courbet, to Venture Independence*, trans. John William Gabriel (New Haven, CT: Yale University Press, 1991), 62–98.

11. Herding, "Equality and Authority," 64.

12. For Herding, this is in direct contrast to the earlier figure paintings, which turned on representational politics that were inherently confrontational. The downsides and weak spots of Herding's totalizing approach are best touched on by Nochlin and Galvez: see Nochlin, "Courbet and His Territory: How Landscape Means," in *Courbet*, 198–99; and Galvez, *Courbet's Landscapes*, 17.

13. Linda Nochlin, "Courbet and His Territory," in *Courbet*, 186–206. This chapter originally took the form of an unpublished 1978 lecture (see *Courbet*, 221n1). For related work on the landscapes and gendered bodies, see Michael Fried, "Courbet's Femininity," in *Courbet's Realism* (Chicago: University of Chicago Press, 1991), 189–222; and Werner Hofmann, "Courbets Wirklichkeiten," in *Courbet und Deutschland*, ed. Werner Hofmann and Klaus Herding, exh. cat. (Cologne: DuMont, 1978), 589–613.

14. Petra ten-Doesschate Chu, "It Took Millions of Years to Compose That Picture," in *Courbet Reconsidered*, ed. Sarah Faunce and Linda Nochlin, exh. cat. (New Haven, CT: Yale University Press, 1988), 55–66. Also germane to the topic is the Musée des Beaux-Arts et d'Archéologie de Besançon's 2000 exhibition and catalogue, Marie-Hélène Lavallée, ed., *Gustave Courbet et la Franche-Comté* (Paris: Somogy, 2000).

15. Petra ten-Doesschate Chu, "Packaging and Marketing Nature," in *The Most Arrogant Man in France: Gustave Courbet and the Nineteenth-Century Media Culture* (Princeton, NJ: Princeton University Press, 2007).

16. Fried, *Courbet's Realism*, 224.

17. Anthea Callen, "Maître Courbet: The Worker-Painter," in *The Work of Art: Plein-Air Painting and Artistic Identity in Nineteenth-Century France* (London: Reaktion, 2015), 105–57.

18. Galvez, *Courbet's Landscapes*, 23.

19. Burgeoning academic interest in the landscapes led to their increasing emphasis in museum exhibitions. The 2000s would see two major shows dedicated entirely to the landscapes: the National Gallery's 2006 *Courbet and the Modern Land-scape* (curated by Mary Morton and Charlotte Eyerman); and the Palazzo Diamanti's *Courbet e la Natura*, see Barbara Guidi, Maria Luisa Pacelli et al., *Courbet e la Natura*, exh. cat. (Ferrara: Ferrara Fondazione arte, 2018).

G. Courbet.

PIGMENT ANALYSIS OF A LANDSCAPE BY GUSTAVE COURBET

ADAM C. FINNEFROCK AND JENNIFER L. MASS

The work examined in this study (**FIG. 11.1**) is a landscape painting on canvas, presumably in oil, that is similar in molecular composition to three works attributed to Gustave Courbet (1819–1877).[1] These three paintings (see, for example, fig. 1.2) were completed in 1864 as part of a series of the rocky grottos and vegetation at the source of the Lison River, a tributary of the Loue River in the former Franche-Comté province of eastern France (now Bourgogne-Franche-Comté).

Preliminary noninvasive elemental analysis was carried out to determine if the palette of the work was consistent with that used by Courbet during his career, which would mean, barring any restoration materials, that none of the pigments, paint additives, or substrate materials should post-date 1877.[2] Analysis of twelve selected areas of the painting did not identify the presence of any anachronistic materials in the work, meaning that pigments and other materials inferred in this study would have been available to artists working in the 1860s.

Courbet's paint palette has not been widely studied or reported. The palette identified by elemental composition of samples from a single painting by Courbet, *The Wounded Man* (*L'Homme blessé*; 1854, Musée d'Orsay, Paris),[3] is consistent with prior research on the artist's work[4] and was compared with the inferred palette of the examined painting. Chemical information and beginning dates of use for possible pigments present in the work were noted. Because no technical analysis of Courbet's palette in the 1860s–70s has been published, it is not possible to

FIG. 11.1 Detail of paint surface and signature in Courbet's *The Source of the Lison* (fig. 1.1).

discern if the potential presence of newer pigments of the period, such as cadmium or cobalt yellow, would be anomalous in the artist's later work. The detection of organic pigments, including anachronistic pigments such as azo dyes or phthalocyanine blue, would require complementary molecular analytical techniques such as Raman spectroscopy and infrared spectroscopy. However, the pigments that can be inferred by X-ray fluorescence analysis would have been available in the 1860s–70s, and so no anachronistic materials are identified. Additional analytical techniques would be necessary to definitively correlate the elements identified with specific compounds within the paint structure (pigments, fillers, ground and preparation layer materials). Analysis of cross-sections taken from the painting would elucidate the stratigraphy of the painting, including the ground and preparatory layers. For his series of Source paintings, Courbet reportedly used a dark ground applied in a thick paste with a palette knife,[5] in contrast to earlier paintings prepared with a calcium-based ground with preparatory layers of lead white mixed with iron oxides and quartz.[6]

This text, an executive summary originally submitted to the University of Pennsylvania on July 30, 2018, as part of Scientific Analysis of Fine Art Report 1760, was edited to conform to the style of the present publication. It is reproduced with permission.

1. The University of Pennsylvania painting that is the subject of this report, and which was subsequently authenticated, measures 18 ⅛ × 21 ⅝ in. (46 × 55 cm). The dimensions of Courbet's Source paintings are variable. Cursory research located only one other work with the same dimensions as the examined painting: *The Saracen Cave* (*La Grotte Sarrazine*), 1864, Musée des Beaux-Arts, Lons-le-Saunier, collection J. L. Mathieu. See Robert Fernier, *La Vie et oeuvre de Gustave Courbet: Catalogue raisonné* (Lausanne: Bibliothèque des arts; Fondation Wildenstein, 1977–78), 1:224 (no. 407). The three similar works to the Penn painting, as listed in Fernier's catalogue raisonné in the 1970s, are *The Source of the Lison* (*La Source de la Lison*; 1864, Collection Galerie Paffrath, Düsseldorf), *Source of the Lison* (*Source du Lison*; 1864, private collection, Switzerland), and *The*

Source of the Lison (*La Source du Lison*; ca. 1864, private collection); see Fernier, *La Vie et oeuvre*, 1:222 (nos. 402, 403) and 2:324 (unnumbered), as *La Source du Lison*, 1864, 61 × 51cm, whereabouts unknown. In 2015, Sotheby's described the latter work as possibly a third version of the composition (in addition to 402 and 403), listed in Fernier's section on unidentified paintings and drawings. Sotheby's, London, *19th Century European Paintings*, auction cat., December 16, 2015, lot 30, http://www.sothebys.com/en/auctions/ecatalogue/2014/19th-century-european-paintings-l15102/lot.30.html.

2. Organic binders and varnish(es) are also present in the paint layers, but are not detected by X-ray fluorescence analysis (XRF). Although XRF may suggest the presence of additives such as metal driers or other inorganic components, this study is focused on the detection of chemical markers indicative of inorganic pigments.

3. Ina Reiche, Myriam Eveno, Katharina Müller, Thomas Calligaro, Laurent Pichon, Eric Laval, Erin Mysak, and Bruno Mottin, "New Insights into the Painting

Stratigraphy of *L'Homme blessé* by Gustave Courbet Combining Scanning Macro-XRF and Confocal Micro-XRF," *Applied Physics A: Materials Science and Processing* 122, no. 11 (2016): 947, https://doi.org/10.1007/s00339-016-0457-1. See also Ina Reiche, Katharina Müller, Erin Mysak, Myriam Eveno, and Bruno Mottin, "Toward a Three-Dimensional Vision of the Different Compositions and the Stratigraphy of the Painting *L'Homme blessé* by G. Courbet: Coupling SEM-EDX and Confocal Micro-XRF," *Applied Physics A: Materials Science and Processing* 121, no. 15 (2015): 903–13, https://doi.org/10.1007/s00339-015-9428-1.

4. Suzy Delbourgo and Lola Faillant, "Courbet, du copiste au maître," *Annales du laboratoire de recherche des musées de France* (1973): 6–20; Bruno Mottin, "A Complete Genesis: Courbet in the Laboratory," in *Gustave Courbet*, ed. Dominique de Font-Réaulx, exh. cat. (New York: Metropolitan Museum of Art, 2008), 70–80.

5. Dominique de Font-Réaulx, "Courbet the Landscapist," in Font-Réaulx, *Gustave Courbet*, 229.

6. Reiche et al., "New Insights."

To translate the customs, the ideas, and the
whole aspect of my time: In one word—
to make a living art—that is my goal.

COURBET IN CONTEXT

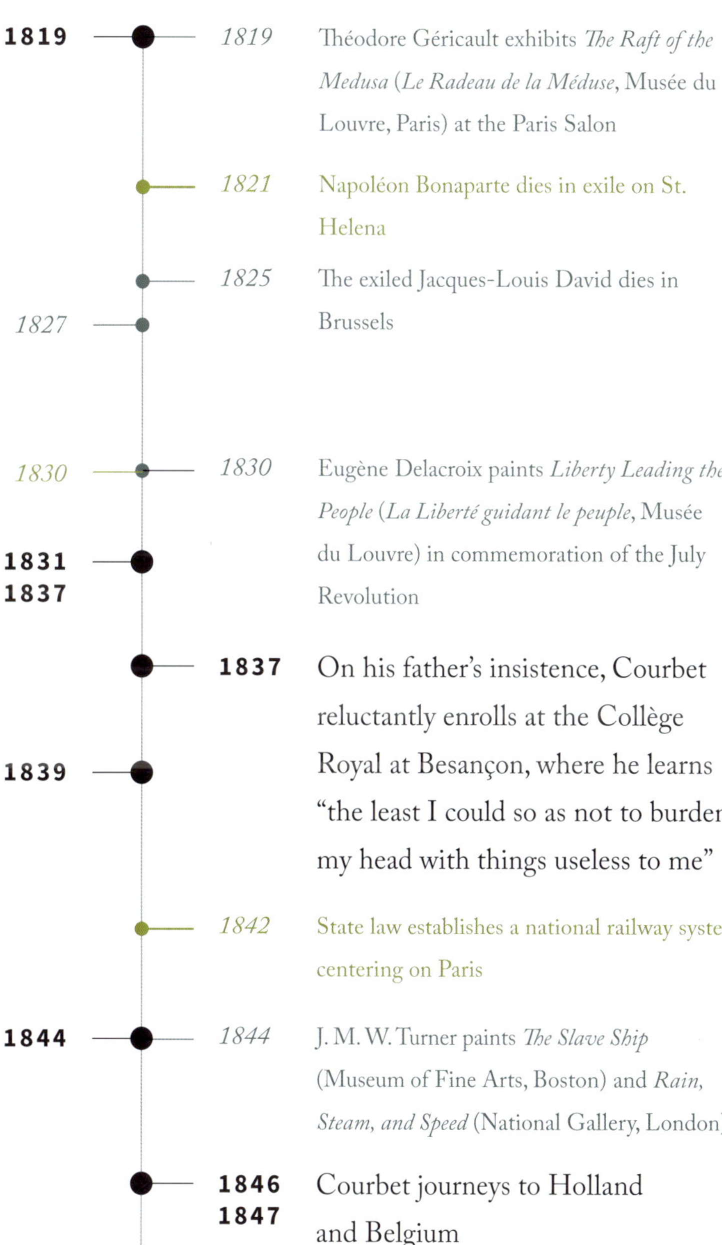

Gustave Courbet is born in Ornans, France, to Régis Courbet, a prominent landowner, and Sylvie Oudot Courbet, a descendant of French revolutionaries

1819 — *1819* Théodore Géricault exhibits *The Raft of the Medusa* (*Le Radeau de la Méduse*, Musée du Louvre, Paris) at the Paris Salon

1821 Napoléon Bonaparte dies in exile on St. Helena

1825 The exiled Jacques-Louis David dies in Brussels

Nicéphore Niépce creates what is widely considered the first photographic image, *View from the Window at Le Gras*

1827

July Revolution

1830 — *1830* Eugène Delacroix paints *Liberty Leading the People* (*La Liberté guidant le peuple*, Musée du Louvre) in commemoration of the July Revolution

Courbet attends courses at the lower seminary of Ornans, where the poet Max Buchon, his life-long friend, is his classmate

1831
1837

1837 On his father's insistence, Courbet reluctantly enrolls at the Collège Royal at Besançon, where he learns "the least I could so as not to burden my head with things useless to me"

Courbet leaves the Franche-Comté for Paris

1839

1842 State law establishes a national railway system centering on Paris

Self-Portrait with a Black Dog (*Autoportrait au chien noir*, Petit Palais, Paris) is Courbet's first canvas accepted by the Salon

1844 — *1844* J. M. W. Turner paints *The Slave Ship* (Museum of Fine Arts, Boston) and *Rain, Steam, and Speed* (National Gallery, London)

1846
1847 Courbet journeys to Holland and Belgium

LEGEND

● Gustave Courbet
● *European Art Historical Events of Note*
● *French Historical Events of Note*

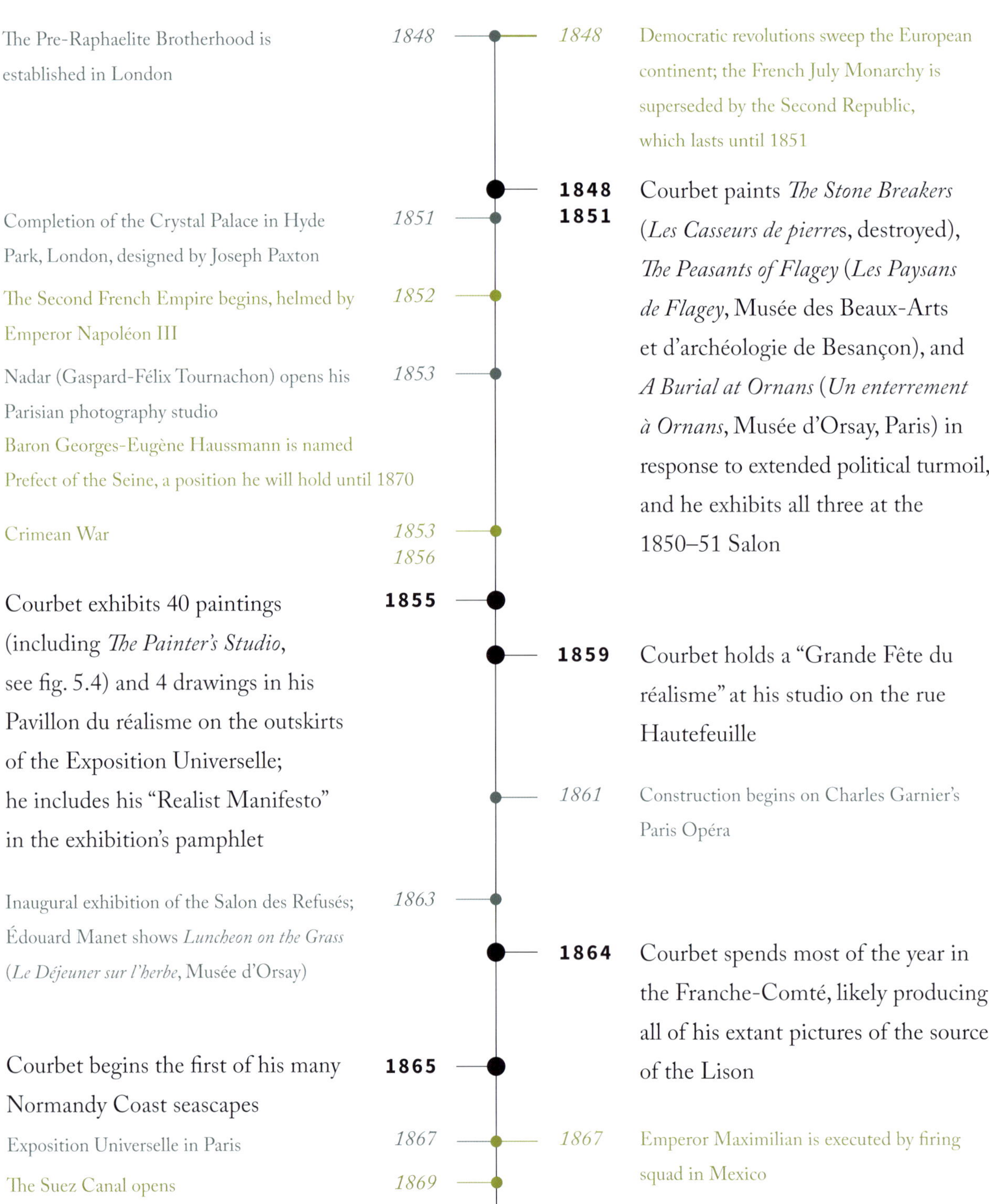

The Pre-Raphaelite Brotherhood is
established in London — *1848*

1848 Democratic revolutions sweep the European
continent; the French July Monarchy is
superseded by the Second Republic,
which lasts until 1851

1848
1851 Courbet paints *The Stone Breakers*
(*Les Casseurs de pierres*, destroyed),
The Peasants of Flagey (*Les Paysans
de Flagey*, Musée des Beaux-Arts
et d'archéologie de Besançon), and
A Burial at Ornans (*Un enterrement
à Ornans*, Musée d'Orsay, Paris) in
response to extended political turmoil,
and he exhibits all three at the
1850–51 Salon

Completion of the Crystal Palace in Hyde
Park, London, designed by Joseph Paxton — *1851*

The Second French Empire begins, helmed by
Emperor Napoléon III — *1852*

Nadar (Gaspard-Félix Tournachon) opens his
Parisian photography studio — *1853*
Baron Georges-Eugène Haussmann is named
Prefect of the Seine, a position he will hold until 1870

Crimean War — *1853*
1856

Courbet exhibits 40 paintings
(including *The Painter's Studio*,
see fig. 5.4) and 4 drawings in his
Pavillon du réalisme on the outskirts
of the Exposition Universelle;
he includes his "Realist Manifesto"
in the exhibition's pamphlet — **1855**

1859 Courbet holds a "Grande Fête du
réalisme" at his studio on the rue
Hautefeuille

1861 Construction begins on Charles Garnier's
Paris Opéra

Inaugural exhibition of the Salon des Refusés;
Édouard Manet shows *Luncheon on the Grass*
(*Le Déjeuner sur l'herbe*, Musée d'Orsay) — *1863*

1864 Courbet spends most of the year in
the Franche-Comté, likely producing
all of his extant pictures of the source
of the Lison

Courbet begins the first of his many
Normandy Coast seascapes — **1865**

Exposition Universelle in Paris — *1867*
1867 Emperor Maximilian is executed by firing
squad in Mexico

The Suez Canal opens — *1869*

LEGEND

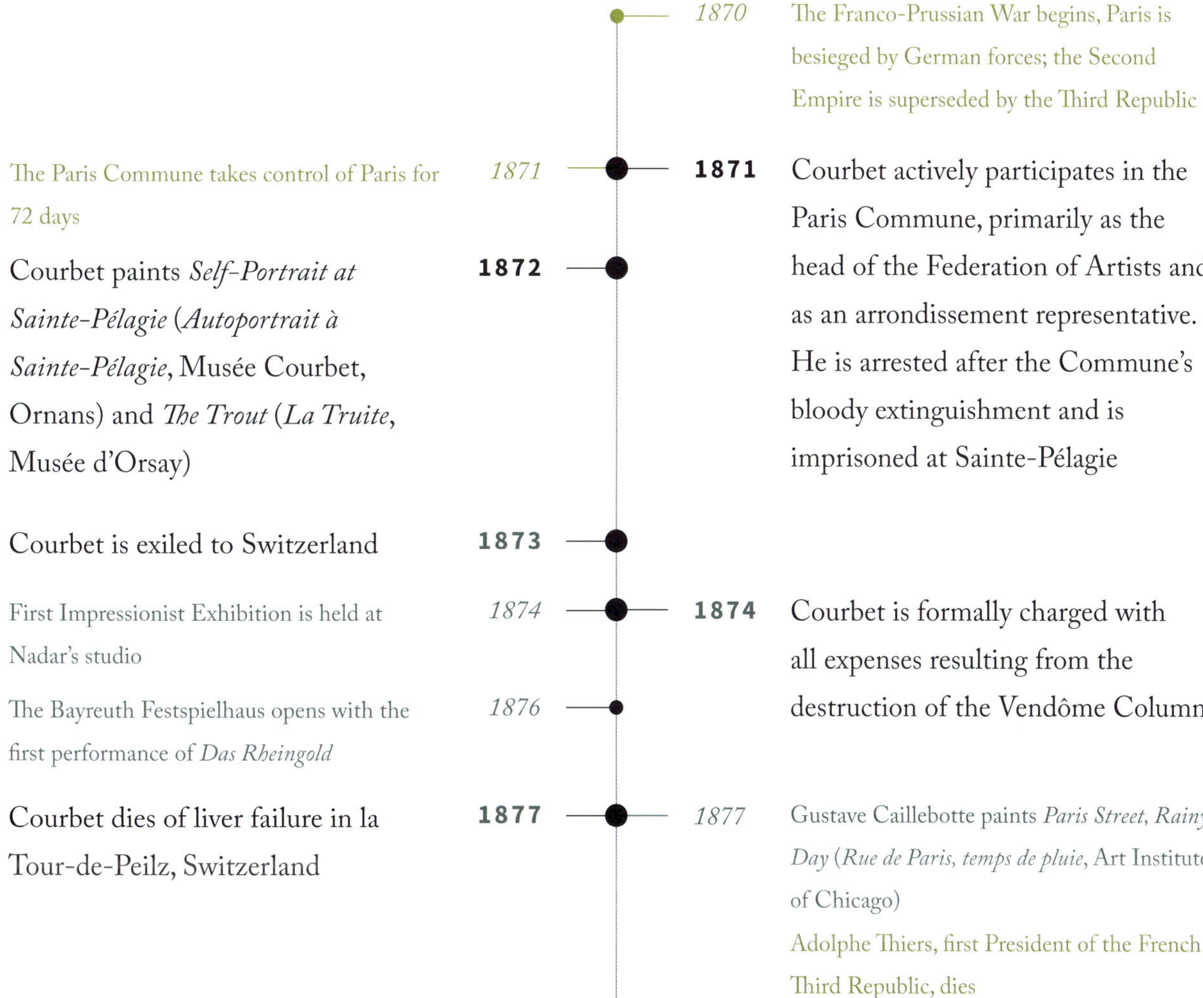
Gustave Courbet
European Art Historical Events of Note
French Historical Events of Note

1870   The Franco-Prussian War begins, Paris is besieged by German forces; the Second Empire is superseded by the Third Republic

The Paris Commune takes control of Paris for 72 days   1871   1871   Courbet actively participates in the Paris Commune, primarily as the head of the Federation of Artists and as an arrondissement representative. He is arrested after the Commune's bloody extinguishment and is imprisoned at Sainte-Pélagie

Courbet paints Self-Portrait at Sainte-Pélagie (Autoportrait à Sainte-Pélagie, Musée Courbet, Ornans) and The Trout (La Truite, Musée d'Orsay)   1872

Courbet is exiled to Switzerland   1873

First Impressionist Exhibition is held at Nadar's studio   1874   1874   Courbet is formally charged with all expenses resulting from the destruction of the Vendôme Column

The Bayreuth Festspielhaus opens with the first performance of Das Rheingold   1876

Courbet dies of liver failure in la Tour-de-Peilz, Switzerland   1877   1877   Gustave Caillebotte paints Paris Street, Rainy Day (Rue de Paris, temps de pluie, Art Institute of Chicago)
Adolphe Thiers, first President of the French Third Republic, dies

EXHIBITION CHECKLIST

PAINTINGS

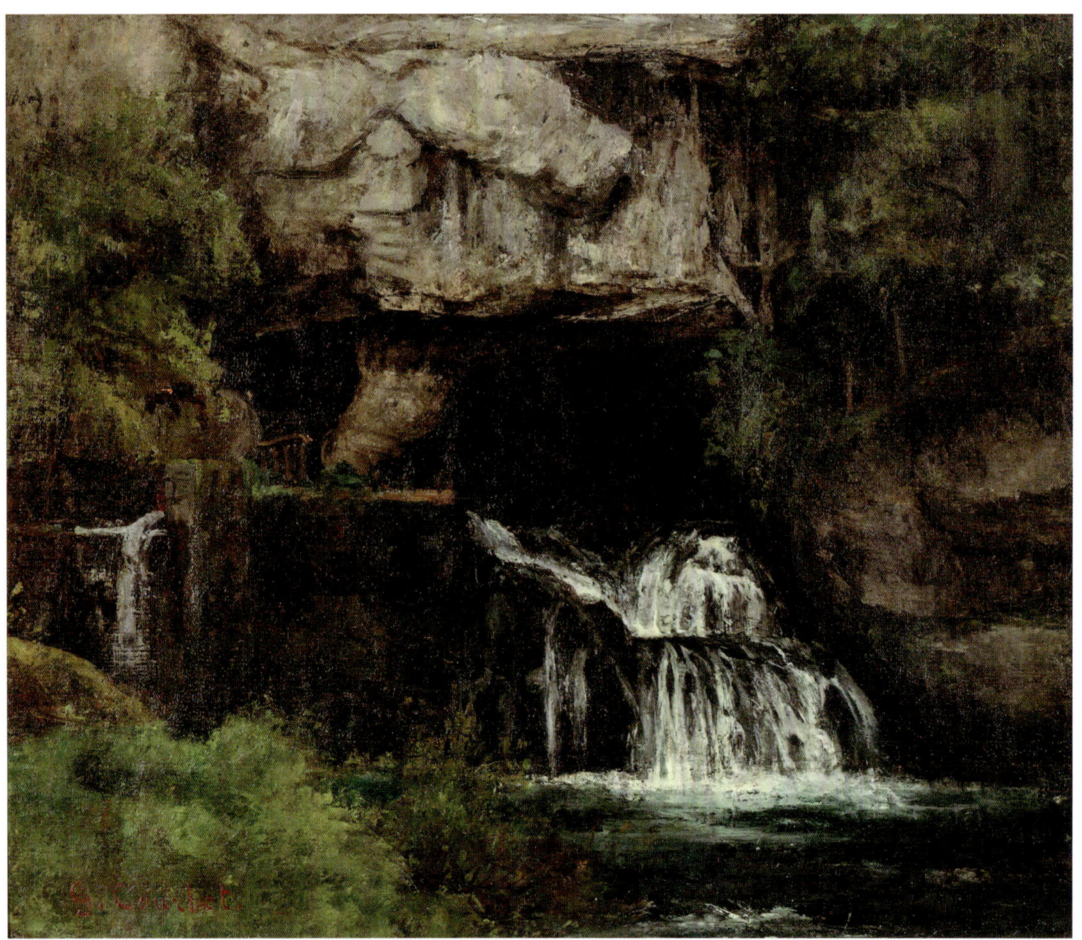

Gustave Courbet (French, 1819–1877)
The Source of the Lison (*La Source du Lison*), 1864
Oil on canvas
18 ½ × 22 in. (46 × 55 cm)
University of Pennsylvania Art Collection,
Gift of Thomas W. Evans
1912.0005.0237

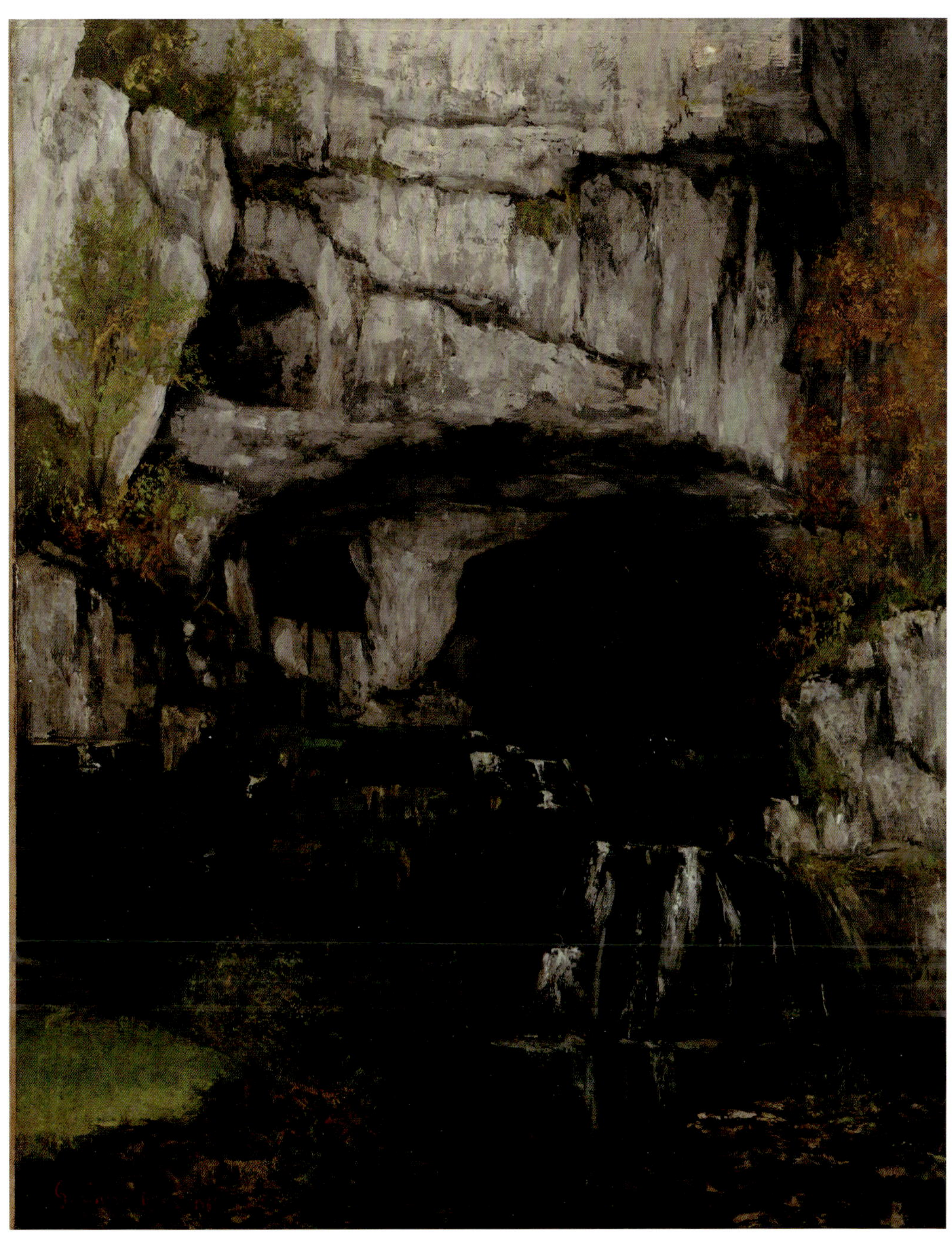

Gustave Courbet
The Source of the Lison (*La Source du Lison*), 1864
Oil on canvas
35 ⅞ × 28 ¾ in. (91.1 × 73 cm)
Private Collection, Minnesota Marine Art
Museum, Winona, Minnesota

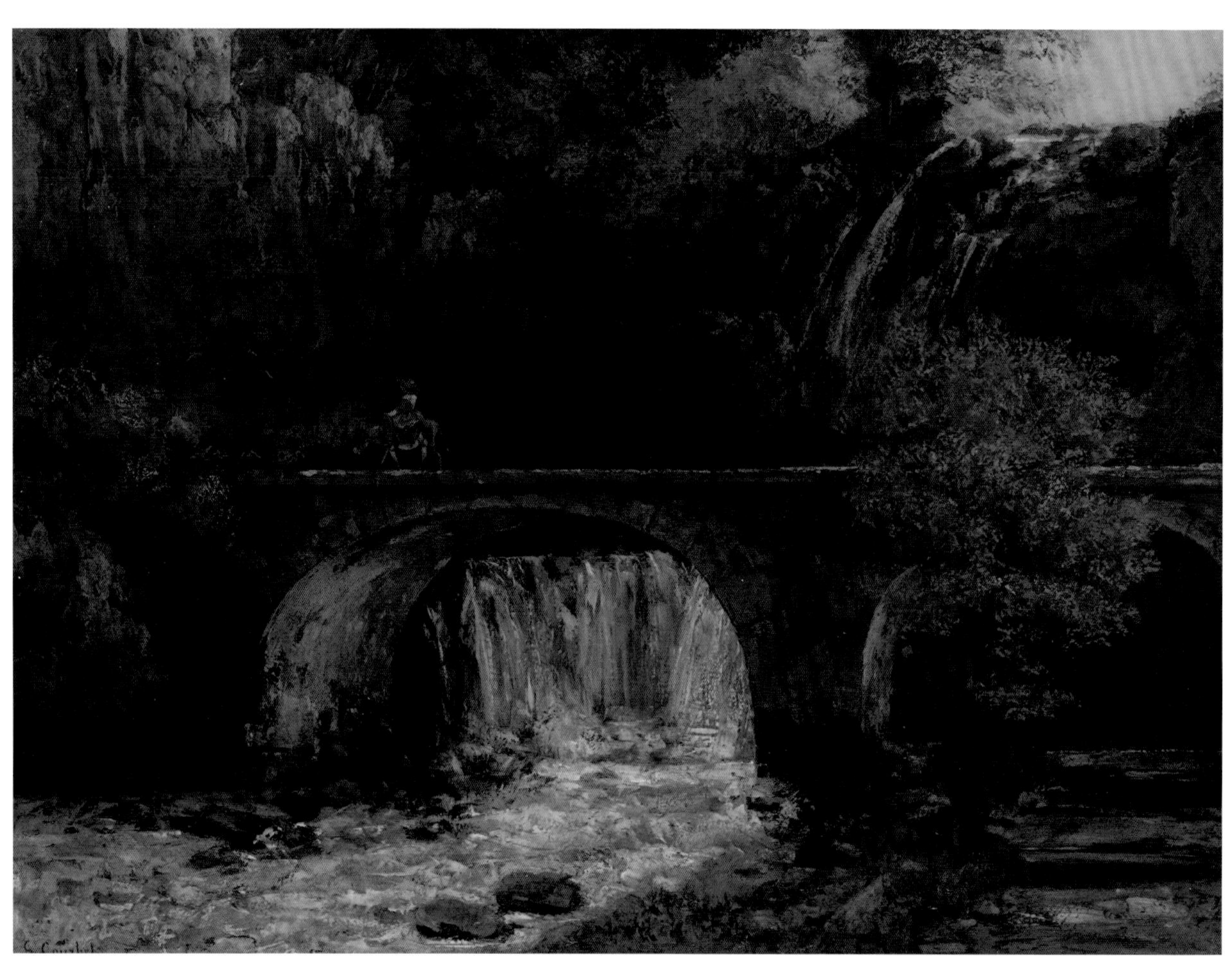

Gustave Courbet
The Great Bridge (Le Grand Pont), 1864
Oil on canvas
37 ⅜ × 50 3/16 in. (95.9 × 127.4 cm)
Yale University Art Gallery, Gift of Dr. and Mrs.
Herbert Schaefer and Mr. Eric Weinmann and
his family
2001.55.1

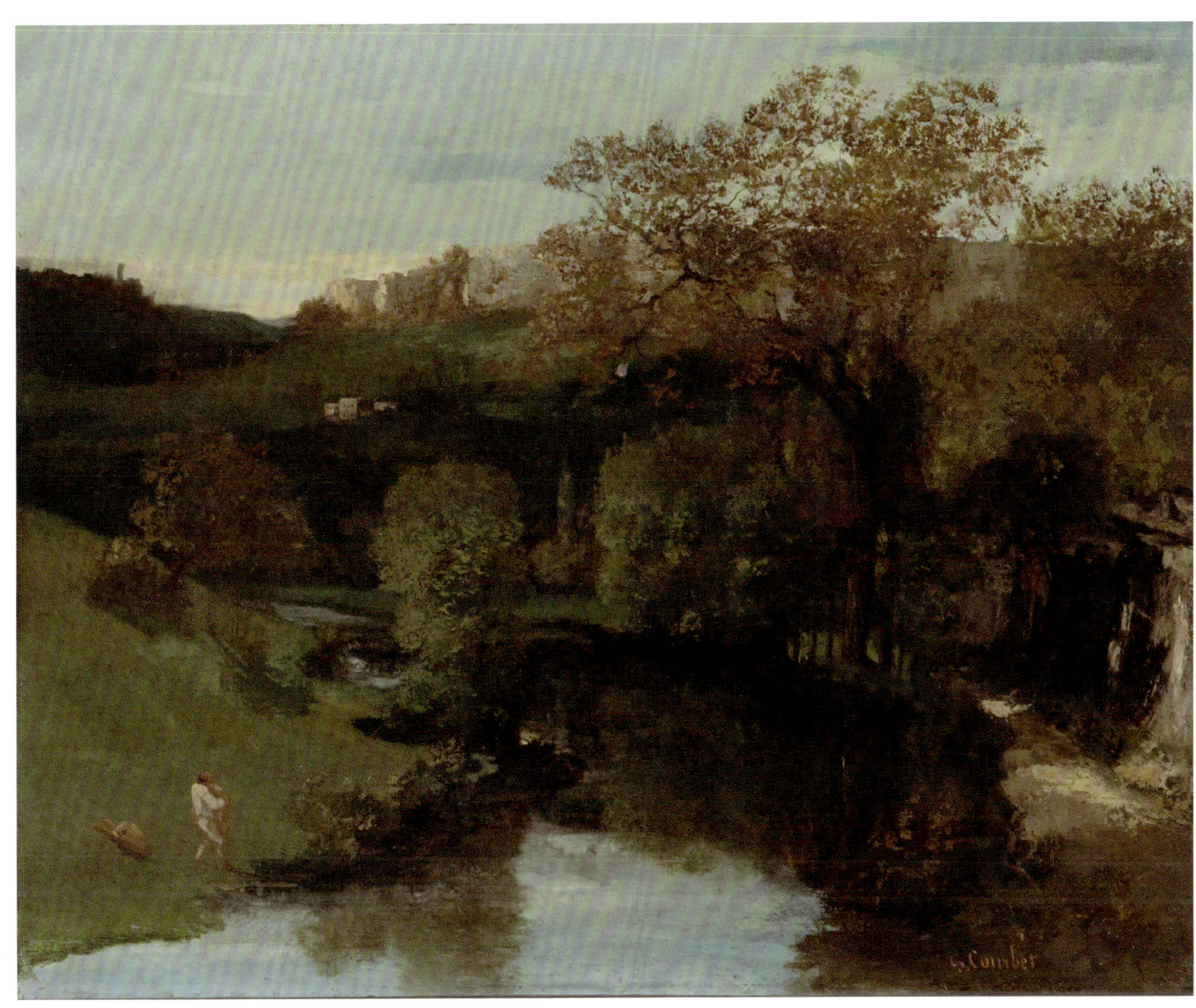

Gustave Courbet
Valley (*La Vallée*), 1857
Oil on canvas
32 × 35 ¾ in. (81.3 × 90.8 cm)
Philadelphia Museum of Art, John G. Johnson
Collection, 1917
942

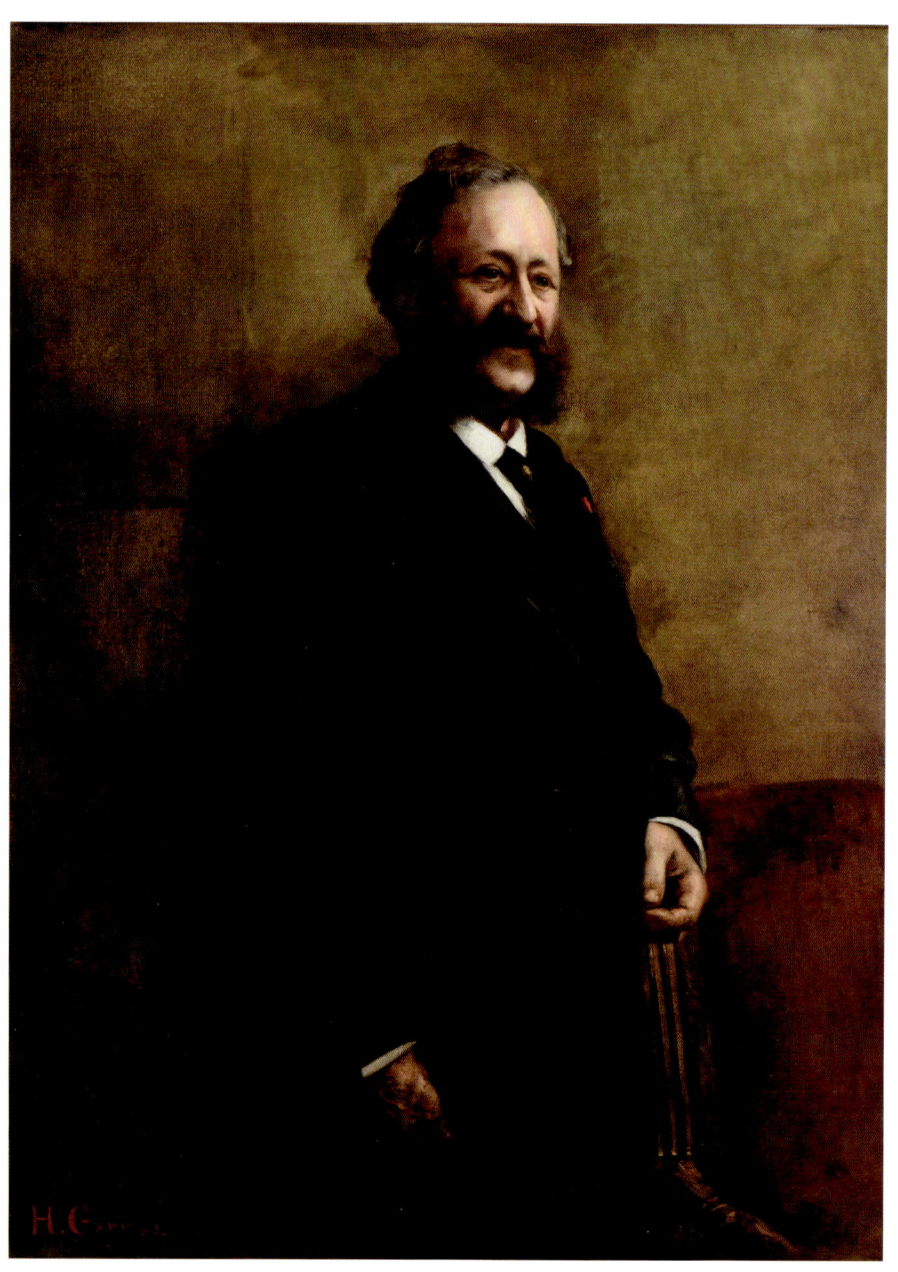

Henri Gervex (1852–1929)
Thomas W. Evans, 1892
Oil on canvas
45 × 34 in. (114.3 × 86.4 cm)
University of Pennsylvania Art Collection,
Gift of Thomas W. Evans
1912.0005.0163

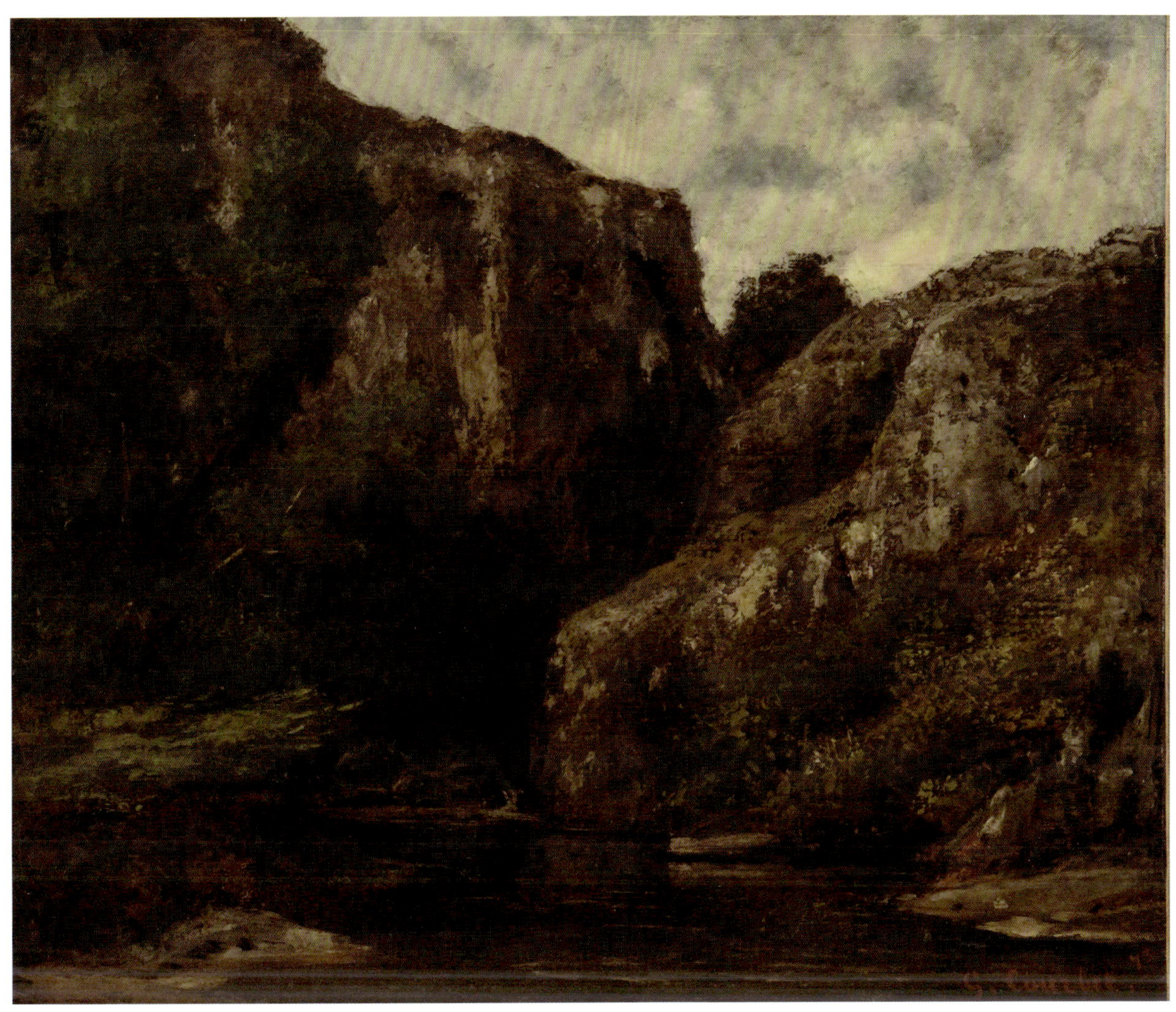

Imitator of Gustave Courbet
Rill in the Mountains, 19th century
Oil on canvas
21 5/16 × 25 9/16 in. (54.7 × 65 cm)
Philadelphia Museum of Art, John G. Johnson
Collection for the W. P. Wilstach Collection, 1907
W1907-1-21

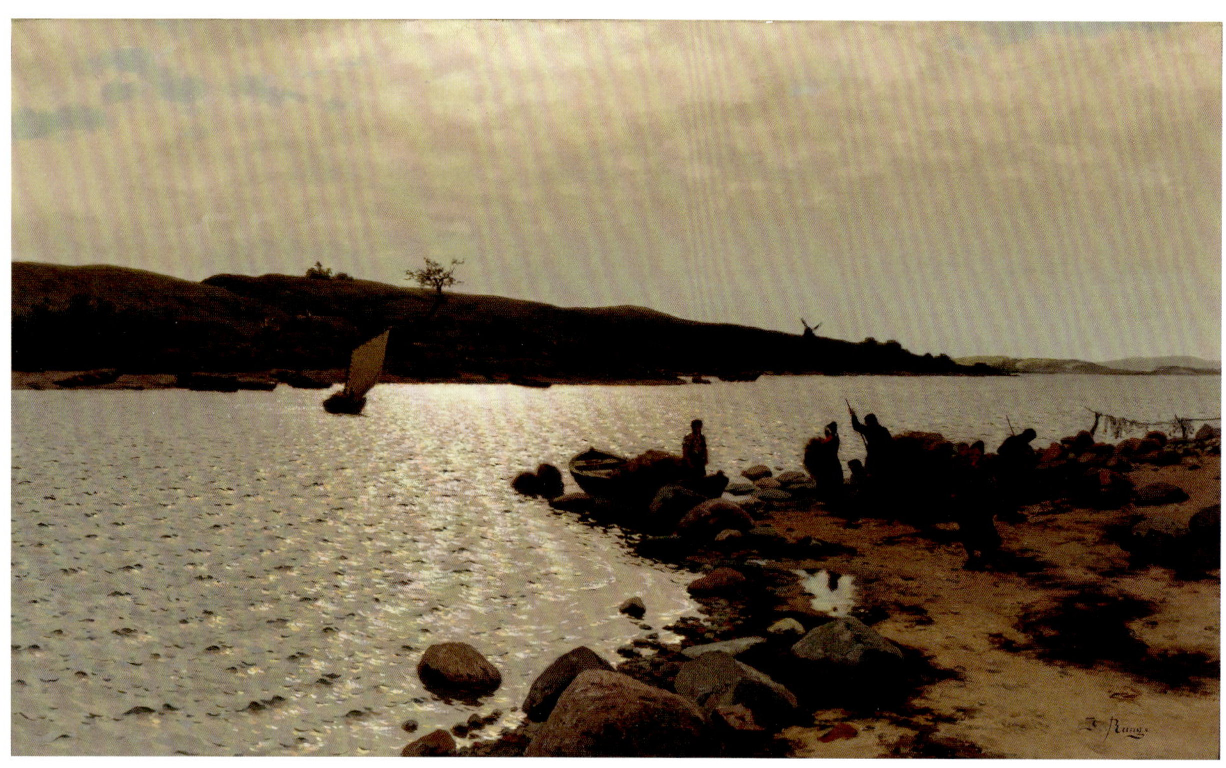

Julius Friedrich Ludwig Runge (1843–1922)
Landscape, 19th century
Oil on canvas
32 ½ × 55 in. (82.6 × 139.7 cm)
University of Pennsylvania Art Collection,
Gift of Thomas W. Evans
1912.0005.0067

"Exhibit 'A,' 6 Janvier 1898," from "Inventaire après
le décès de M. le Docteur Evans"
Ink on paper
Closed: 12 ¼ × 8 ⅞ × ⅜ in. (22.9 × 31 × 1 cm)
Open: 12 ¼ × 17 ¾ × ¾ in. (22.9 × 45.1 × 2 cm)
Kislak Center for Special Collections, Rare Books
and Manuscripts, University of Pennsylvania
See fig. 2.4

Charles Nodier (1780–1844),
Isidore-Justin-Séverin Taylor (1789–1879),
and Achille-Alexandre-Alphonse de Cailloux de
Cailleux (1788–1876)
*Voyages pittoresques et romantiques dans l'ancienne
France*, volume 2, *Franche-Comté*
Paris: P. Didot l'aîné, 1825
Printed book with engravings
21 ¼ × 14 ⅜ × 2 ¹⁵⁄₁₆ in. (54 × 36.5 × 7.5 cm)
The National Gallery of Art Library, Victoria and
Roger Sant Fund
See figs. 4.2, 6.2

Société géologique de France (founded 1830)
Mémoires de la Société géologique de France,
volume 3, part 1
Paris: P. Bertrand, 1848
Journal
13 ¼ × 10 in. (34.3 × 25.4 cm)
University of Pennsylvania Art Collection

"No. 299. Nans-sous-Ste. Anne (Doubs). La Source
du Lison (altit. 390 m.)," n.d.
Librairie David-Mauvas à Salins, Jura, France
Postcard
3 ½ × 5 ½ in. (8.9 × 14 cm)
University of Pennsylvania Art Collection

"Sites Pittoresques de Franche-Comté: 1258.
Environs de Salins-les-Bains. Nans-sous-Sainte-
Anne—Source du Lison," n.d.
Établissements C. Lardier, Besançon
Postcard
3 ½ × 5 ½ in. (8.9 × 14 cm)
Collection of Petra ten-Doesschate Chu

"St. Martin-de-Bavel, vue générale aérienne," n.d.
Éditions aériennes Combier imp. Mâcon
Postcard
4 × 5 ½ in. (10.2 × 14 cm)
University of Pennsylvania Art Collection

"Sites Pittoresques de Franche-Comté C.L.B. 1203.
Environs de Salins-les-Bains (Jura). Nans-sous-Ste.
Anne, La Grotte de la Source du Lison," n.d.
Publisher unknown
Postcard
3 ½ × 5 ½ in. (8.9 × 14 cm)
University of Pennsylvania Art Collection

"La Grotte de la Source du Lison," n.d.
Publisher unknown
Postcard
6 ½ × 4 ½ in. (16.5 × 11.4 cm)
University of Pennsylvania Art Collection

FURTHER READING

Callen, Anthea. *Courbet*. London: Jupiter, 1980.

———. "Maître Courbet: The Worker-Painter."
In *The Work of Art: Plein-Air Painting and Artistic Identity in Nineteenth-Century France*, 105–57.
London: Reaktion, 2015.

Chu, Petra ten-Doesschate. "Courbet or Not Courbet, That Is the Question." *IFAR Journal* 7, no. 1 (September 2004): 18–26.

———. *The Most Arrogant Man in France: Gustave Courbet and the Nineteenth-Century Media Culture*. Princeton, NJ: Princeton University Press, 2007.

Clark, T. J. *Image of the People: Gustave Courbet and the 1848 Revolution*. 3rd ed. Berkeley: University of California Press, 1999.

Clarke, Michael. "Courbet: Peintre des paysages." In *Courbet: Artiste et promoteur de son oeuvre*, edited by Jörg Zutter and Petra ten-Doesschate Chu, 83–100. Paris: Flammarion, 1998. Exhibition catalogue, Musée Cantonal des Beaux-arts, Lausanne, November 1998–February 1999; and Stockholm National Museum, March–May 1999.

Courbet, Gustave. *Letters of Gustave Courbet*. Edited and translated by Petra ten-Doesschate Chu. Chicago: University of Chicago Press, 1992.

Faunce, Sarah, and Linda Nochlin, eds. *Courbet Reconsidered*. New Haven, CT: Yale University Press, 1988. Exhibition catalogue, Brooklyn Museum, November 1988–January 1989; and Minneapolis Museum of Art, February–April 1989.

Font-Réaulx, Dominique de, ed. *Gustave Courbet*. New York: Metropolitan Museum of Art, 2008. Exhibition catalogue, Grand Palais, Paris, October 2007–January 2008; Metropolitan Museum of Art, New York, February–May 2008; and Musée Fabre, Montpellier, June–September 2008.

Fried, Michael. *Courbet's Realism*. Chicago: University of Chicago Press, 1991.

Galvez, Paul. *Courbet's Landscapes: The Origins of Modern Painting*. New Haven, CT: Yale University Press, 2022.

Green, Nicholas. *The Spectacle of Nature: Landscape and Bourgeois Culture in Nineteenth-Century France*. Manchester: Manchester University Press, 1990.

Guidi, Barbara, Maria Luisa Pacelli et al. *Courbet e la Natura*. Ferrara: Ferrara Fondazione arte, 2018. Exhibition catalogue, Palazzo dei Diamanti, September 2018–January 2019.

Herding, Klaus. *Courbet, to Venture Independence*. Translated by John William Gabriel. New Haven, CT: Yale University Press, 1991.

Hofmann, Werner, et al. *Courbet und Deutschland*. Cologne: DuMont, 1978. Exhibition catalogue, Hamburger Kunsthalle, Hamburg, October–December 1978; and Städelsches Kunstinstitut, Frankfurt, January–March 1979.

Joly, Carine, Valerie Pugin et al. *Gustave Courbet: L'École de la Nature | The School of Nature*. Sivana: Cinisello Balsamo, 2021. Exhibition catalogue, Musée de l'Abbaye, Saint-Claude, January–April 2021.

Lavallée, Marie-Hélène, ed. *Gustave Courbet et la Franche-Comté*. Paris: Somogy, 2000. Exhibition catalogue, Musée des Beaux-Arts et d'Archéologie de Besançon, September–December 2000.

Le Men, Ségolène. *Courbet*. New York: Abbeville, 2008.

Morton, Mary, ed. *Looking at the Landscapes: Courbet and Modernism. Papers from a Symposium Held at the J. Paul Getty Museum on March 18, 2006*. J. Paul Getty Museum: Online publication, https://www.getty.edu/publications/virtuallibrary/0892369272.html?imprint=jpgt.

Morton, Mary, and Charlotte Eyerman, eds. *Courbet and the Modern Landscape*. Los Angeles: Getty Publications, 2006. Exhibition catalogue, J. Paul Getty Museum, Los Angeles, February–May 2006; Museum of Fine Arts, Houston, June–September 2006; and the Walters Art Museum, Baltimore, October 2006–January 2007.

Nochlin, Linda. *Courbet*. New York: Thames & Hudson, 2007.

Rubin, James. *Realism and Social Vision in Courbet and Proudhon*. Princeton, NJ: Princeton University Press, 1980.

Stöppel, Daniela. "Courbets Repliken: Erschaffung und Aufhebung des Originals in der Kopie." In *Wiederholungstäter: Die Selbstwiederholung als künstlerische Praxis in der Moderne*, edited by Verena Krieger and Sophia Stang, 29–47. Cologne: Böhlau Verlag, 2017.

Thomas-Maurin, Frédérique, ed. *Sensations de nature: De Courbet à Hartung*. Paris: Lineart, 2015. Exhibition catalogue, Musée Courbet, Ornans, July–October 2015.

Wagner, Anne. "Courbet's Landscapes and Their Markets," *Art History* 4, no. 4 (1981): 410–31.

Young, Marnin. *Realism in the Age of Impressionism: Painting and the Politics of Time*. New Haven, CT: Yale University Press, 2015.

6ᵉ année. — N° 18   Un numéro 10 centimes   13 juin 1867

LE HANNETON

ILLUSTRÉ, SATIRIQUE ET LITTÉRAIRE
PARAISSANT LE JEUDI

Rédacteur en chef : VICTOR AZAM   Directeur : EUGÈNE VERMERSCH

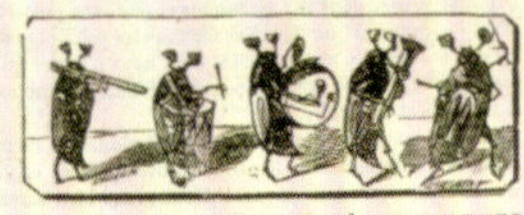

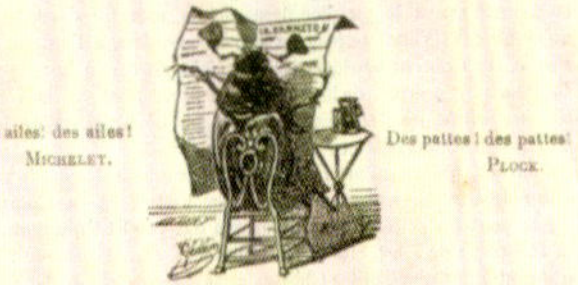

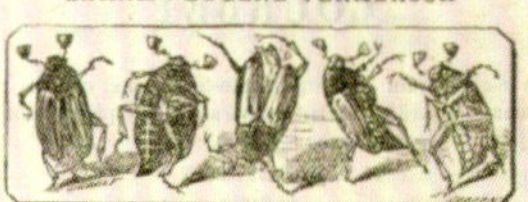

PARIS
Un an............. 5 fr. »
Six mois.......... 3 »
Trois mois........ 1 50

DÉPARTEMENTS
Un an............. 6 fr. »
Six mois.......... 3 50
Trois mois........ 2 »

BUREAUX : Rue de Trévise, 37

PARIS
Un an............. 5 fr. »
Six mois.......... 3 »
Trois mois........ 1 50

DÉPARTEMENTS
Un an............. 6 fr. »
Six mois.......... 3 50
Trois mois........ 2 »

G. COURBET, PAR L. PETIT

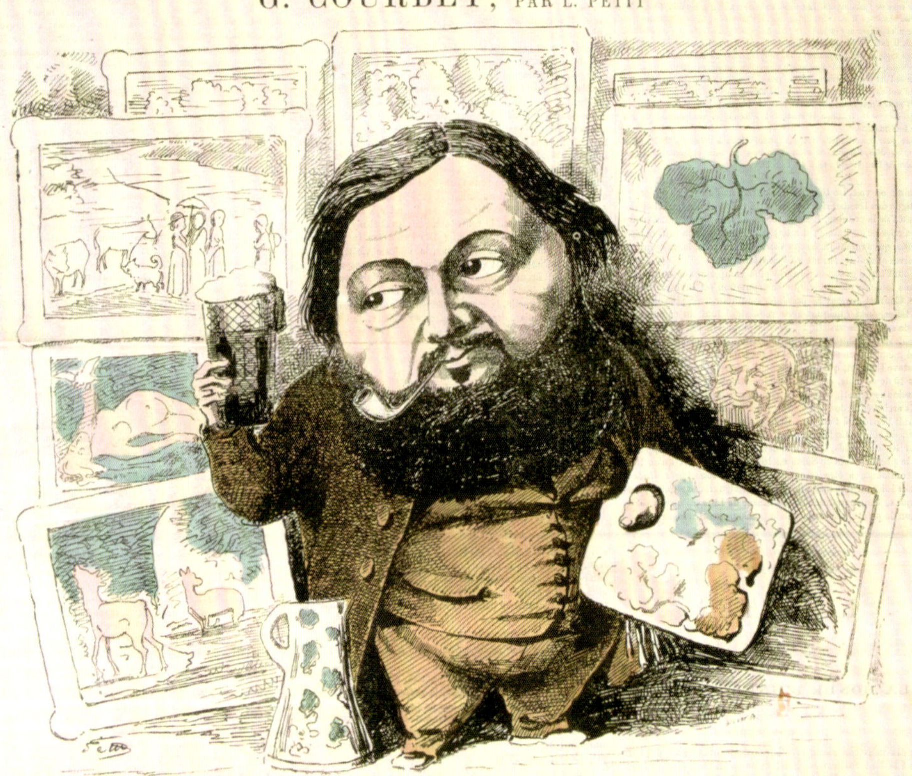

CONTRIBUTORS

LYNN MARSDEN-ATLASS has been the executive director of the Arthur Ross Gallery since 2008 and curator of the University of Pennsylvania Art Collection since 2010. She has curated thirty-four exhibitions at the Arthur Ross Gallery. Previously, she served as senior curator of the Pennsylvania Academy of the Fine Arts, curator of American and contemporary art at the Chrysler Museum of Art, associate director and registrar of the Colby College Museum of Art, and director of the Consortium of Colleges Abroad in Paris. She was professor of nineteenth-century French art for the British Institute in Paris and three colleges, as well as adjunct professor in the Départment d'anglais at Université de Caen in 1992–93. In 2016, she was an affiliated fellow at the American Academy in Rome.

ANDRÉ DOMBROWSKI is Frances Shapiro-Weitzenhoffer Associate Professor of 19th-Century European Art at the University of Pennsylvania, specializing in the arts and material cultures of France and Germany in the late nineteenth century. Author of *Cézanne, Murder, and Modern Life* (2013), a book about the artist's early work, he has also written essays on Manet, Monet, Degas, Pissarro, and Menzel, among others. He is the editor of the *Wiley Companion to Impressionism* (2021), bringing together thirty-four essays on Impressionism. He is currently working on his next book, tentatively titled *Monet's Minutes*, rooting the rise of the impressionist instant—and nineteenth-century painting's presumed new "quickness" more

OPPOSITE Léonce Justin Alexandre Petit, *G. Courbet*, cover of *Le Hanneton* (Paris), June 13, 1867. Private collection.

broadly—in the period's innovative time technologies and forms of time management.

JALEN CHANG is a PhD candidate in the history of art at the University of Pennsylvania and the 2022–23 Carl Zigrosser Fellow at the Philadelphia Museum of Art. A graduate of the Williams College / Clark Art Institute Master's Program in Art History, he is preparing a dissertation on the revolutionary and imperial politics of nineteenth-century drawing regimens.

PETRA TEN-DOESSCHATE CHU, a specialist in the history of nineteenth-century European art, has published extensively in this area. She is the author of the widely used college textbook *Nineteenth-Century European Art*, currently in its third edition, and one of the two founding editors of *Nineteenth-Century Art Worldwide* (19thc-artworldwide.org), an electronic journal devoted to the art of this period. Chair of the Art History and Museum Studies Department at Seton Hall University for twenty-one years, she cofounded, with Professor Emeritus Barbara Cate, the Master of Arts Program in Museum Professions.

ARUNA D'SOUZA regularly writes for *4Columns* and the *New York Times*. She is the author of *Cézanne's Bathers: Biography and the Erotics of Paint* (2009) and *Whitewalling: Art, Race, and Protest in 3 Acts* (2018), which was named one of the best art books of 2018 by Holland Cotter in the *New York Times*. She is the editor of Linda Nochlin's *Making It Modern: Essays on the Art of the Now* (2022) and of Lorraine O'Grady's *Writing in Space 1973–2018* (2020). Other editorial projects include *The Invisible Flâneuse?: Gender, Public Space and Visual Culture in Nineteenth Century Paris* (2008, with Tom McDonough) and *Art History in the Wake of the Global Turn* (2014, with Jill H. Casid). She co-curated, with Catherine Morris, *Lorraine O'Grady: Both/ And*, which opened at the Brooklyn Museum in March 2021.

ADAM C. FINNEFROCK is the vice president of Scientific Analysis of Fine Art, LLC (SAFA), a global scientific consulting firm that addresses questions about artworks' attribution, state of preservation, provenance, and mechanisms of degradation. In carrying out this work, SAFA assists art conservators, museums, art lawyers, auction houses, and art insurers in their cultural heritage preservation missions. Adam is a research physicist with expertise in laboratory and synchrotron x-ray techniques, spectroscopic microanalysis, and novel technologies including hyperspectral imaging and machine learning/artificial intelligence.

PAUL GALVEZ is an art historian, critic, and curator, and was most recently a research associate at the Edith O'Donnell Institute of Art History at the University of Texas, Dallas, where he was also director of the Masters of Arts Program in Art History. He is the author of *Courbet's Landscapes: The Origins of Modern Painting* (2022), and his writings have appeared in *Art Journal, October, Cahiers du Musée national de l'art moderne, Texte zur Kunst* and *Artforum*.

JENNIFER L. MASS is the president and founder of Scientific Analysis of Fine Art, LLC (SAFA), a global scientific consulting firm that addresses questions about artworks' attribution, state of preservation, provenance, and mechanisms of degradation. In carrying out this work, SAFA assists art conservators, museums, art lawyers, auction houses, and art insurers in their cultural heritage preservation missions. Mass is also professor of cultural heritage science at Bard Graduate Center.

MARY MORTON is curator and head of the French Paintings Department at the National Gallery of Art (NGA) in Washington, DC. She began her curatorial career in the European Art Department at the Museum of Fine Arts, Houston, then served as associate curator of paintings at the J. Paul Getty Museum in Los Angeles. Her exhibition projects prior to arriving at the NGA include *Courbet and the Modern*

Landscape (2006), *Oudry's Painted Menagerie* (2007), and *The Spectacular Art of Jean-Léon Gérôme* (2010). At the NGA, she organized the presentation of *Gauguin: Maker of Myth* (2011), a reinstallation of the gallery's renowned nineteenth-century collection (2012), *Gustave Caillebotte: The Painter's Eye* (2015), *Cézanne Portraits* (2017–18), *Corot Women* (2018), and *True to Nature: Open-Air Painting in Europe*, 1780–1870 (2020). In 2018, the French government awarded her Chevalier of the Order of Arts and Letters.

EMILY ZIMMERMAN is a curator and writer based in Philadelphia. She is currently the assistant director / assistant curator of the Arthur Ross Gallery at the University of Pennsylvania. Previously, she was the director and curator of the Jacob Lawrence Gallery at the University of Washington, and she has held positions at the Henry Art Gallery and the Experimental Media and Performing Arts Center (EMPAC) at Rensselaer Polytechnic Institute, among others.

PHOTOGRAPHY CREDITS

Photo by Jaime Alvarez: fig. 2.1; pp. 116, 118

© Archives Charmet / Bridgeman Images: fig. 8.2

Courtesy of Art Institute Chicago: fig. 9.7

Photo by Petra Chu: fig. 3.3

Photo by Madeleine Coursaget: fig. 6.3

Courtesy of Getty Research Institute: fig. 9.1

Courtesy of Google Arts and Culture: fig. 9.8

Photo: HIP / Art Resource, NY: p. 122

Photo by Mitro Hood: fig. 5.5

Courtesy of Institute Gustave Courbet: p. v

Photo by Andres Kilger: fig. 1.1

Photo by Thierry Le Mage. © RMN-Grand Palais / Art Resource, NY: figs. 4.4, 7.1

Photo by Hervé Lewandowski © RMN-Grand Palais / Art Resource, NY: figs. 5.4, 7.3

Courtesy of Metropolitan Museum of Art, New York: fig. 9.4

© Musée départemental Gustave Courbet / Photo by Pierre Guenat: fig. 10.1

© National Museums Liverpool / Purchased with the aid of the National Art Collections Fund 1961 / Bridgeman Images: fig. 5.6

Photo by Franck Raux. © RMN-Grand Palais / Art Resource, NY: fig. 4.3

Photo by Luisa Ricciarini / Bridgeman Images: fig. 3.4

Courtesy of the State Library of Victoria: fig. 2.2

Courtesy of Wikimedia Commons: figs. 9.3, 9.6